The American Nightmare

The American Nightmare

Why Inequality Persists

CLARICE STASZ

Schocken Books · New York

First published by Schocken Books 1981
10 9 8 7 6 5 4 3 2 1   81 82 83 84

Library of Congress Cataloging in Publication Data

Stasz, Clarice.
  The American nightmare.

  Includes index.
  1. Discrimination in employment—United States.
2. United States—Social policy. I. Title.
HD4903.5.U58S72   331.13′3′0973   80–6191

Designed by Judith F. Warm
Manufactured in the United States of America
ISBN 0–8052–3765–8

Contents

To the memory of
Martin Luther King, Jr.,
whose dream is worth remembering

Acknowledgments

In 1977, I received a fellowship from the National Endowment for the Humanities to attend a year-long seminar at Brown University on "The Black American Experience." For independent study I planned to examine the role of black women in the United States, the contrast between the way they define themselves and the way others see them; however, upon my first visit to the library I found few books by or about black women. That this disturbing omission could occur at a school reputed to be among the best in the country seemed sharp testimony to the myopic way we define educational quality.

I began to think over my own sociological training, one that prepared me to know a very narrow band of society, the life of success-oriented white males, with the intimation that their world was the only one worth knowing. In recent years I had challenged that view by studying the role of women, so I decided to take this year's freedom to add a similar survey of the lives of racial minorities, white ethnics, and others of disadvantage in our society. My plunge into this awesome task would never have been made without the sensitive support of Richard Quinney. He was the ideal colleague: patiently listened to false enthusiasm, offered cheer during confusion, and asked the question that would force order out of muddled thought.

Fellow seminar members pointed me toward solutions of unwieldy issues, and responded to several chapters of the manuscript. These commentators include Susan Blake, Thadious Davis, Trudier Harris, David Helwig, Rhett Jones, Harold Pfautz, and the elusive but stimulating Josiah Carberry. Further resources were provided in the summer of 1978 by the Center for Social Organization of Schools, Johns Hopkins University, whose members were unearthing many facts that supported my speculations. I am particularly grateful to Edward MacDill, James McPartland, and Linda Gottfredson. Richard Johnson of the University of Washington was generous in answering requests concerning historical sources. None of these people fully support my interpretations, nor are they responsible for any errors contained herein.

Others bolstered me during troublesome times of the writing, especially Ann Weingarten Zimmer, Frederick Walsh, Richard Bellamy, and Gaye Robbins. By travelling to Wales, Averil and John Anderson left me the necessary writer's den, while Milo Shepard, Jean Carnahan, and "V" Pratt made sure I was not lonely during the hideaway days in Sonoma.

I am grateful to the administrators of Sonoma State University who permitted extra leaves of absence, to the students in my management classes who disputed and debated my ideas, to my colleagues in the sociology department who voiced encouragement, and to the librarians, who have secured an outstanding collection, unusual for a small school, and who responded to all special requests quickly.

My agents, Elizabeth Pomada and Michael Larsen, by their guidance, example, and confidence in my work, and by their immediate response to any matter—be it a cheer of encouragement or the red-pencilling of a passage—gave me a rich apprenticeship in the craft of writing.

Through a few, succinct suggestions, editor John Simon guided me away from a needless pedantic rhetoric to a more direct voice.

Kathy Baker proved the writer's ideal—a typist who called out problems in the text before reproducing them.

Though Kendra complained about the noise of the typewriter and the burnt vegetables, she never asked me to stop writing.

Taking advantage of Mercury in transit, Michael Orton chose precisely the right moment to unlock doors never touched before.

Introduction

Poverty disappeared during the seventies in America, slipping from sight so smoothly that no one took notice to hold a self-congratulatory celebration. But the miracle had happened.

If a 1967 civil-rights activist had been transported by time machine to the year 1980, and confined to a room furnished with a television set and chair, she would have concluded from her new view of the country that the poor were no longer with us. In his State of the Union address that year, President Carter directed his most detailed comments to foreign affairs, military defense needs, and energy. In later speeches on the economy, he would discuss the fat in government, wage-and-price controls, and again, energy. The familiar sixties rhetoric about hungry Americans, ill-housed Americans was not to be heard from in other branches of Washington either.

Even Ted Kennedy, out on some mysterious vendetta against the president, failed to make the impassioned speeches on behalf of the poor that rang in the past from his assassinated brothers. Unemployment was a problem; Kennedy repeatedly demanded large funds of money toward government-sponsored jobs. Yet this unemployment was not tied to any particular underdog group in the society, but toward the reversal of recession. During his appearances, Kennedy was not surrounded, as his brothers had been, by articulate, charismatic spokespersons for the poor. And though 481 black delegates attended the Democratic convention, none appeared at a special caucus meeting on black concerns. One could only deduce that the poor were few in number.

Few whispers of discontent were heard during the celebrations at the Republican convention that year. That party's platform committee voted by 90 to 9 to remove support for the Equal Rights Amendment for women from its platform. Yet female delegates voiced satisfaction to reporters for that decision, suggesting that women's progress was on schedule. And for the first time the convention body included a visible representation of minority groups—a strange sight for a party traditionally composed of affluent whites. Black delegates spoke hopefully of drawing their kinspeople's votes away from the Democrats, and seemed unconcerned that they had nominated a man known for beliefs such as this one: "Unemployment insurance is a prepaid vacation plan for freeloaders."

Among these odd circumstances was yet another, the presence of a strong independent candidate, John Anderson. Surely, if there were a poor, he as the spoiler candidate might be their representative. But his stands were an amalgam of disagreements with the regular party standard bearers; his only strong civil rights position was on behalf of women.

Clearly a new spirit had suffused the country, one that covered all political corners. People were digging in their heels, shifting toward the right. Jimmy Carter's economic plans sounded increasingly like those of previous Republican administrations.

The economy was foremost in people's minds—talk resounded daily of runaway inflation, recession, stagflation, even depression—and they spoke as though the troubles touched everyone equally. It was as if everyone were middle-class and having trouble making ends meet. To bring up words like "the poor" or "discrimination" seemed embarrassing, as if to mention a ne'er-do-well from the family's past. The country was having too many difficulties deciding how to keep its automobiles running and its home furnaces burning, to raise any ancient spectres.

Though the sources of this shift in orientation are too complex to detail here, it helps to see the transformation in one major group of actors during the period, the influential intelligentsia. In the late sixties, men well-placed in government, journalism, and the university reexamined their political beliefs, and concluded that the liberalism of the civil rights period was fraught with error. Irving Kristol, Nathan Glazer, Norman Podhoretz, Daniel Bell, Daniel Patrick Moynihan, Edward Banfield, James S. Coleman, James Q. Wilson, Seymour Martin Lipset—most had been in the forefront of social liberalism a few short years before. For example, Coleman had directed the major study in support of school desegregation, while Moynihan had served as an influential reformer in New York politics. Prolific writers, powerfully positioned, these men served as advisors to officeholders, drafted legislation, served on special commissions, commentated on news affairs programs, and ghosted speeches. They appeared on the covers of *Time* and enjoyed frequent attention in the very journals and newspapers they criticized as being liberal monopolies. Some of these men knew one another, and doubtless directly influenced one another's changing views, but in general their doubts about recent reforms seemed the result of independent, thoughtful reflection.

It was easy for a fiercely objective person to question and wonder what was going on. The American left had become intellectually flabby. Its appeal struck more at the emotions than the realities: you were pure if you didn't put down blacks, farm workers, and students. Women of the left added their sex to the list (although the men had a hard time incorporating this addition to their platform). Simple conspiracy theories abounded: police were pigs, capitalists were pigs, generals were monsters, and politicians were dumb and untrustworthy. Blue-collar whites were ridiculed as violent and racist. In California, a gang of thugs who had murdered a well-liked black school superintendent and shot at bystanders during bank robberies became heroes when they kidnapped an heiress. Many stupid ideas rode the banner of a once-elegant Marxism.

While the left was very good at demonstration and mass emotional display, in its day-to-day activities a lack of real-politik crippled it from ensuring profound, lasting reforms. Fractionalization forced odd personal decisions: should the black woman side with her men as a race or join the white woman in the struggle against sexism? Leaders emerged on the basis of bravado, machismo, and celebrity appeal, not the ability to administer a movement through a long time of struggle and frustration. Liberals romantically overestimated the effectiveness of the new laws they created, and were blind to the reactionary potential of government bureaucracy.

At their worst, leftists became smug and self-righteous, believing themselves to be the only persons in society with heart and feeling. They could come out with curiously antidemocratic thoughts, for example, discount any expressions from the working class (especially white ethnics) that did not fit their preconceived dogma on oppression. They ignored the class split in their own movement, the irony of white intellectuals researching the poor or marching in the South, only to return to the comforts of the university at the start of a new semester.

Though the left's vision of America was perceptive and often uncomfortably accurate, one which stimulated important changes in equal opportunity, its social order was fragile, ill-shaped, and divided. Following the coronation of Richard M. Nixon, it lost its momentum. People tired of public displays, grew preoccupied with the winning of the war, and at the success of that effort, found the economy much less fluid and adaptable than in the sixties.

The emergent critics of the left quickly devised an alternative—eventually dubbed neoconservatism—that appealed to many Americans, especially those who felt they had been treated shabbily by the social activists. The theoretical strength of this new ideology rests in its ability to forge a coalition among once disparate groups.

One major theme among the writings of neoconservatives is the discrediting of social inequality as a problem. It is not so much that the writers deny its existence, for they fill their arguments with relevant statistics, so much as they say the problem is not so bad as liberals had claimed, and that anyway, nothing can be done about it. By sketching a world of great complexity, they appeal to those who feel alienated and without moral order in their lives. It is ironic that so many neoconservatives are social scientists; by definition, they surely should be able to communicate models by which to make sense of that world. Instead, they suggest it is a world beyond comprehension, even for men as brilliant as themselves, and naturally conclude that one had best let it go on its own relentless way rather than interfere. This allows them to declare such social policies as the "benign neglect" of minorities or the dismantling of governmental agencies concerned with energy, health, and consumer protection.

Another theme appeals to those disturbed by the loss of traditional values in American society—the breakup of the family, the unconcern with children's welfare, the attacks on churches, the absence of genuine patriotism. It is particularly here that neoconservatives attract a large base, because people in disadvantaged positions share the distress of middle-class whites over the erosion of values. In a society rife with violence, greed, and dishonesty, the desire for a morally upright order readily attaches itself to any political affiliation. Another constituency is the fundamentalist revival, which draws so heavily on the poor and anonymous, and encourages people to put aside material need to replace it with a struggle over evil and corruption.

While this increase in morality is laudable, it is a position tarnished by various accompanying beliefs—that the poor are shiftless and lazy, that women who seek careers are family destroyers. The country is thought to be threatened by an underclass—a scum of the ineducable, unemployable, and immoral. Furthermore, it is argued that this rabble is being directed and misled by the writings of "Know-Everythings"—liberal academics, persons who lack religious ties, are indifferent to home and kin, and care little for the lives of decent, hard-working, honest people. Thus self-righteousness infects neoconservative beliefs, resurrecting racism, sexism, and anti-intellectualism.

The neoconservatives tempt through their guaranteeing an end to the fear of being mediocre or average. They argue against egalitarian schemes, for everyone would, in Kristol's words, only "end up with equal shares of everything." A society without hierarchy eludes them. The rich are to be envied, emulated; the poor serve to give the rest of us something to look down upon.

As with any ideology, neoconservatism plays off some truths, and its observations are at times telling. An example is in the writings of affirmative action. As this book will demonstrate, many neoconservative claims here are fallacious. Yet the writers have correctly pointed out the unfair treatment of parts of white society, notably ethnics and rural inhabitants. Looking over the social activism of the sixties, there is no denying that these people, who compose the bulk of the poor in our society, were passed over, that some features of affirmative action as it is practiced today only add to the disadvantage of these white working-class people. The neoconservative error is in making the issue of inequality a racial one, when it is based rather in the organization of work and wealth in our society.

Though neoconservatives announced the death of poverty, they fostered a mass hallucination, a convenient denial of reality. The word is gone, yet the substance remains.

Consider some statistics.

While Republicans caucused and cheered their unusual party unity, one out of five workers in the surrounding streets of Detroit was looking for a job. In some inner cities, one out of two able-bodied, motivated black youths was unable to find work. Overall in the summer of 1980, the National Jobless Rate hovered at 7.8% (twice the "acceptable" rate of 4%) for a total of 8,200,000 Americans who worried daily how they were going to pay the rent and the grocer's credit. Though news commentators and government experts implied this unemployment was a general result of inflation, underneath could be found the buttresses built by that longtime enemy, discrimination. The jobless were the once familiar disadvantaged groups—persons of color, women, recent immigrants, the aged, people with disabilities. Their unemployment was an old story, though few spoke it anymore.

The affluent America, the land where everyone was getting the basic needs and freedom from want, was another figment in this new vision. In 1980, the richest ten percent of the country stuffed into their bank accounts one-third of all personal income and almost sixty percent of national wealth; the poorest ten percent divided up thin portions from one percent of all personal income, and was in debt. Inflation could hardly have the same significance for those top ten as for the ninety underneath. In fact, the wealthy further benefited from their discretionary income, for example, by investing in housing, driving up its value, and pricing the average American out of the market.

Besides discrimination, other problems in the work life of Americans persisted. During the seventies, workers repeatedly told social researchers that their major complaint on the job was not pay or benefits, but unsafe and unhealthy conditions. About eight of every ten reported worry over physical injury or chronic illness as a result of their job environments. Workers felt increasingly unhappy, out of control over their labor, useless, bored, tired, or depressed. Not surprisingly, government labor experts discovered that fully half of all workers were in positions where the required skills were inferior to the capabilities and education of the job holders. This suggests a deplorable waste of talent—people capable of responsible and creative work not being given the opportunity.

In discounting these facts the new conservatism affirms that social issues are secondary to economic ones. If necessary, high levels of unemployment are to be tolerated to cool down runaway inflation. Investment sources—businesses and the well-to-do—should be granted tax relief to stimulate their spending in capital growth. Labor is encouraged to temper its demands and work harder. The country's resources are argued to be too strained to allow more expense on welfare relief, additional worker benefits, job safety implementation, equal opportunity programs, and the like. As the most "liberal" of the 1980 politicians, Ted Kennedy, stated, people need jobs before anything else.

The separation of social from economic issues imperils the nation. By discounting the seriousness of discrimination, poverty, and work dissatisfaction, the new conservatism ignores their fundamental contribution to current economic ills. When two men labor daily at jobs with responsibility and skill, but one by virtue of job title earns three times as much as the other, the privileged worker has funds to outbid and price up goods the less well-paid worker desires and deserves. When the majority of all workers are in dead-end jobs, they are prone to boredom, lack of interest in craft, desultoriness, and unconcern with productivity. When the members of a neighborhood group find themselves shunted to poorly paid work, their smaller paychecks rebound throughout their community: restaurants close, plumbers and painters make fewer repairs, and shopkeepers hover at bankruptcy.

To simply make jobs for people is of little long-run value if those jobs are designed and rewarded as they have been in the past, with outmoded personnel practices in reign. Eight million jobs in 1980 might have settled the economy temporarily, but, like the tobacco that eases nervousness today, would have produced malignant destruction later, for the divisions that are at the base of our ills would only be hardened.

Underlying the refusal to recognize the signs of distress is a determination to preserve the American Dream. This ethos, uplifting in its hopefulness, ineluctable for its dramatic line of challenge, conquest (and for some, tragic failure), traps each of us in illusion. However bad the struggle for necessities and pleasures in these crazy economic times, we each want to believe that we may one day escape, that determination and effort will be charged by enough luck to place us on Easy Street. This vaunted opportunity, this glow of redemption, distracts and tempts us in our daily lives from meditation upon potential unities within the country, from the egalitarian virtues that have slipped from fashion.

Perhaps the defenses are healthy. The recent years of venality and incompetence in government leave us maturely and appropriately cynical. Americans are smarter than politicians and self-appointed experts presume—certainly no one candidate would win in many elections these days, were "none of the above" a ballot option. But to pull inward and decide to pay attention only to one's own life is foolhardy. This determined individualism allows the ineffective to continue in power and those with vociferous stances to have an influence out of proportion to their numbers and reason. The future portends poorly unless we pause to consider the values upon which this country was founded, ones which promise equality as well as opportunity, social welfare as well as the pursuit of private wants.

It is this purpose, to return to the old-fashioned social criticism of the sixties, that concerns the present book. While the topic is dear to social liberals, the analysis and recommended solutions know no political home. Though conservatives err through their poor economics and preoccupation with meritocracy, they nonetheless understand something of the positive uses of individualism as a motivating appeal. Though liberals are quick to acknowledge the harsh struggle of life among the disadvantaged, they fail to appreciate why government agencies and employers with the best intentions do not comply with equal-opportunity policies. Though radicals have the clearest view of the labor market, they offer little more in way of solution than inspirational calls for the workers to unite. It is in transcending these orthodoxies that a new criticism can be reached, one that suggests fresh social and economic policies—some mundane, some outrageous—but all practical and practicable, with promise of drawing the country closer to our founding ancestors' ideals.

The American
Nightmare

Chapter 1

The Dream
Depraved

The American myth is of free will in its simple, primary sense. One can choose oneself and will oneself; and this absurdly optimistic assumption so dominates the republic that it has bred all its gross social injustices. "All men are born equal" becomes "No decent society can help those who fail to stay equal."
                                    John Fowles, **Daniel Martin**

On any schoolday, children around the United States pledge their allegiance to the republic, which stands, "one nation, under God, indivisible, with liberty and justice for all." History books tell them that the country sprang from a revolution against an autocratic, monarchical power, a mother country that did not want to treat the colonies with equal justice. The implication is that the new lands were a place where all could be equal under God and government, where freedom was the birthright of each citizen.

That the colonies themselves did not provide equal treatment to its people has, with the exception of slavery, been overlooked by civics texts. That this inequality continues to the present time is denied. That many of the children who make this oath themselves face injustice is ignored. Pledging daily, they mature to believe their words; as adults they rationalize or deny evidence that the social order is not consistent with their patriotic rhetoric. Curiously, even those who suffer injustice, and see so clearly, share many of the same values as those in privileged positions.

Whatever their lot in life, contemporary Americans are likely to affirm a belief in individual achievement, even though this means some persons will end up with more rewards than others. They would agree with the imagery of a nineteenth-

3

century success tract: Life is a tollway along which both the poor and the wealthy must pay the same fees in order to reach a destination lush with material comforts. This is in contrast to other Western countries, where aristocracy and place at birth leave some with more roads to choose from than others, and fewer costs along the journey as well. In the United States, the fees are measured not in money or familial connections, but in human effort and perseverance. Thus the arrangement is held to be an egalitarian one, not because all are equal at the end of the journey, but because all travel the same roads. This model of achievement forms the theme for a complex mythology often referred to as the American Dream.

PURITANICAL PARADOX

The roots of the dream are long and twisted, reaching down to the earliest layers of Colonial society with its Puritanical soil. Despite their common and simple appearances, the Puritans were not a consistent lot. Their attitudes toward life and society were fraught with paradoxes. In early New England, just as "the angels stood in serried ranks," so too did humans, under God, live in a state where "some to be High and Honourable, seem to be Low and Despicable, some to be Monarchs Kings, Princes and Governeurs, Masters and Commanders, others to be subjects, and to be commanded, servants of sundry sorts and degrees, bound to obey; yea, some born to be slaves, and so to remain during their lives, as have been proved. Otherwise there would be a meer parity among men."[1] And a "meer parity" was an abomination of the natural order, a most feared possibility.

Though preferring a society with hierarchies, the Puritans perceived its structure as basically egalitarian for several reasons. First, as Thomas Hooker explained, "Mutuall subjection is as it were the sinewes of society, by which it is sustained and supported."[2] This doctrine bound each person equally to another person of superior rank, student to teacher, teacher to schoolboardsman, schoolboardsman to governor, governor to God. Most important, those in the upper ranks were under an inescapable injunction to serve those beneath them, or the public at large. The Puritan gentleman or lady was not to pursue a life of leisure or self-indulgence.

Second, if the upper ranks had obligations, the lower ones had rights. Supreme among these was that inferiors were to be treated with respect, and were worthy of self-esteem. Since it was in the natural order of things that some be inferior, they were not to be held responsible for their lowly position. No one was inherently superior or inferior, but only as one stood in relation to another person in a particular situation. Those of "meene place and calling" would find their consolation in considering that by their performance of "poore and base duties" they were serving God.[3] Though no lawful calling should be despised, those with wealth, education, or social standing were honor bound to aspire to important positions, and to earn greater rewards in the form of goods, money, and services.

Such attitudes produced a social order which perpetuated inequality. Yet, given the motive that people should devote themselves diligently to their duties, to unceasingly and systematically pursue their livelihoods for the greater glory of God, the system included the seeds of its own destruction. A well-kept ledger was the sign of religious virtue in its keeper, but it also helped him to be more successful in his business. Since neither riches nor social status were evil, for they were to be shared with the community, they could be accumulated with little guilt. Hence the Puritans gave their followers the impossible task of immersing themselves in the things of the world, yet not settling their affections upon them.

Within several generations of their arrival in the New World, one observer wrote of the prevalence of "novelties, oppression, atheisme, excesse, superfluity, idelness, contempt of authority."[4] Yet even this worldliness fit into the theology, for one advantage of becoming rich was the opportunity to declare how debased one had become, to denounce one's self as unfaithful, tempted by covetousness. To be really happy, the Puritans would have had to create a society in which they could earn money without rising into wealth, or lose it without falling into poverty.

On the other side, poverty was not an affliction to be feared, because it presented opportunities for spiritual advancement. One judged one's spiritual growth not by one's rewards or afflictions so much as the uses one made of them. Just as the man of talent was to apply himself industriously and efficiently to the increase of his measure, so too poverty provided one with the opportunity to overcome adversity.

Still, if the Puritans did not consider the poor to be sinners, they nonetheless resented contributing to their support. Consequently, the treatment of the poor tended to be severe toward "idlers," and included jailing, eviction from a town, or the binding out of children of indigent families as apprentices or servants. At the same time, the "worthy poor" could expect some charities, and persons of means often made bequests for charitable uses. Consequently, though pure religious doctrine held the poor were not to be blamed, in fact some were treated otherwise.

Given a society with such a strong sense of subordination, inequality, authority and suppression of individual will, it must seem puzzling that a revolution could spring from its soil. The reason rests partly with other practices the Puritans introduced into their social order.[5] First, unlike the Old World, the differences in wealth were small. In a land with much natural resource and a chronic labor shortage, most people could manage a comfortable standard of living. And those of privilege had nowhere the amount or variety of luxuries enjoyed by the aristocracy of England.

Farmers owned their land outright rather than serving as tenants to a noble. Governors ruled as the ultimate authority, but they were to receive the assurance of that power through frequent public elections. Ministers held little civic authority, being unable (as their European brethren were) to hold office. Religious leaders told individuals to follow their calling for the glory of God, but the parishioners could see around them many opportunities to enjoy in this world the glories of earth. Consequently, the society offered the fulfillment of hopes and wishes that could be only fantasies to average people in the Old World.

INDIVIDUALISM EMERGENT

As the colonies grew in area and population, so too did social inequality. While early Puritan society had been led by a small prosperous class, the bulk of it consisted of middle-class property owners. By the 1800s, however, more variations in class structure appeared.[6] In frontier locations, equality predominated, with farmers, artisans, merchants, and a few professionals sharing similar standards of living in remote outpost communities. However, in the cities and commercial farming areas where most of the populace dwelled, a few families controlled businesses, land, and banking, and many people struggled to meet basic needs.

Patterns of immigration established finer variations in social status and life style. Most obvious was the importation of slaves for commercial farming. Besides creating a class of disenfranchised citizens, slavery set white farmers themselves into a class system. Ten percent of Southern farms owned more than half the land; forty percent of Southern white men were landless, forming a class of dependent laborers. Throughout the colonies, other white persons—perhaps as many as one in three—entered as indentured servants, and had to work out contracts to become free and independent wage earners.

While the rich accumulated ever larger proportions of land, luxury, and leisure, the poor found ever fewer pieces of cloth and crusts of bread.[7] Although the cities were the places a man could best fulfill ambitious dreams, they were also uncongenial settings for those who failed. Being most frustrated by the clogged channels of mobility, the middle class recognized the growing stasis in the society and supported the egalitarian ideals that eventually provoked revolutionary actions. As one New Jersey journalist in 1780 noted, there were too many people "who by reason of their wealth or education, or titles, think themselves above the common sort of people. . . . Such men, so superior in their own conceit, would, if they had favourable opportunity, bring others into subjection and slavery. But equality should be encouraged."[8] And so it was.

The revolution temporarily reversed trends toward inequality by enfranchising all white men, allowing them to own property, and forbidding the use of titles. It astonished the world by guaranteeing that the United States was a country where any white male could improve his social and economic position without legal impediments.

It is not surprising, then, that during this time one man became the first well-publicized symbol for the ideal of social achievement in American society. Benjamin Franklin, the seventeenth child of a Boston soap chandler, rose to share the company of royalty.[9] As a printer in his early years, Franklin spoke through the "Poor Richard" of his *Almanack* to preach virtues of discipline, industry, efficiency, frugality, and other Puritanical ideals:

> *Have you somewhat to do To-morrow, do it Today.*
>
> *The Sleeping Fox catches no Poultry.*
>
> *The Cat in Gloves catches no Mice.*
>
> *Silks and Sattins, Scarlet and Velvets, put out the Kitchen Fire.*

As an old man, fattened from achievement, Franklin self-consciously shaped his autobiography to instruct the young on the means to success, both by good example and by warning. There he emphasized the importance of cultivating both the reality and appearance of virtue, for example, to live modestly rather than to flaunt one's means. Self-interest, he believed, would persuade people to act with integrity, for others would prefer genuinely benevolent acts to flattery. Thus Franklin agreed with the Puritans that advancement was to serve humanity.

In fact, Franklin's successes arose from other than his own efforts.[10] While young, he had the sense to leave class-frozen Boston for the socially open city of Philadelphia. As one of the few printers there he was able to meet most people in positions of power. His craft led him to be given the post of legislative clerk, which left him privy to major political decisions. When he saw a need in the city, be it military defense, quality education, fire protection, or library services, he initiated organizations to meet each need, establishing important social connections and acquiring public popularity in the process. During Franklin's time, doubtless many others had his character, but few were so well-placed for advancement. (And as it happens, Franklin was among the first to admit in private that he was not the industrious, efficient man Poor Richard urged upon his readers.)

Through manipulation of his public *persona*, Franklin supplanted the worship of God as the motive for achievement with a humanistic morality. A man with a zesty enthusiasm for earthly pleasures, he assured others that, Puritans to the contrary, it was not sinful to enjoy the rewards of hard work in this life. The game of individual success-seeking became worthy in itself.

Thus, the Constitution provided the citizenry with the idea of an egalitarian society tempered by a cultural doctrine—unspoken of in legal tracts—of individual incentive. Hopes prevailed that class distinctions would end and prosperity spread to all. Unlike pre-Revolutionary days, there were no religious tests to inhibit achievement (and unlike later, no corporate monopolies). At the close of the century Noah Webster wrote with hyperbole, "Here every man finds employment, and the road is open for the poorest citizen to amass wealth by labor and economy, and by his talent and virtue to raise himself to the highest offices of this State."[11]

THE SELF-MADE MAN

It has been an American conceit that the self-made man originated on our shores, when in fact other societies have provided special channels for advancement independent of inheritance or nobility. Perhaps it is more accurate to say that nowhere has a culture so enshrined and worshipped this idea as the United States did during the 1800s. In the first decades of the century, the expanding Western frontier fulfilled the dreams of those pioneers courageous enough to seek them. By 1830, the emerging urban economy and move toward industrialization thrust out new ledges for the ambitious poor to climb toward and

cling to. Later, with the close of the Civil War, yet another set
of opportunities for business acquisition pushed up from the
economy, offering more spaces in the higher levels of the hierarchy.

During this century, the American dream of success became
fully secularized and earthbound. As in previous eras, certain
activities were held by clergymen, writers, and businessmen to
be both virtuous and necessary for success, among these self-
reliance, industry, perseverance, and sobriety.[12] Talent was of
little import; character was primary. Indeed, genius was even
deprecated by the many writers of the success mythology.
"The genius which has accomplished great things in the world,
as a rule, is the genius for downright hard work, persistent
drudgery," wrote one.[13] What mattered was to develop habits
that would please employers: punctuality, reliability, good
cheer during adversity, obedience, initiative, and the willingness to work extra hours without pay.

The voices for these ideals were widespread. School children
read in their McGuffey readers, "The road to wealth, to honor,
to usefulness, and happiness, is open to all, and all who will,
may enter upon it with the almost certain prospect of success."[14] For their leisure reading, many youths turned to one of
the 107 novels of Horatio Alger, Jr., who prodded boys to work
hard, avoid dissipation, and thus be in the position for luck to
thrust them into prominence.[15]

Adult readers were most likely to pick from the shelves of
inspirational novels, usually Christian in tone, that exhorted
them to behave with uprightness and decency, and thus reap
material successes as well as spiritual benefits. By the turn of
the century, the public would find such literary stars as Theodore Dreiser, Jack London, and Frank Norris extolling the success myth as the key to the meaning of American life.[16] Then
too, vulgarizations of William James's writings (known as the
"New Thought") would teach readers that they were not limited in any absolute sense, but could effectively will themselves
to succeed.[17]

Like the Puritans, the aspiring self-made men were advised
to follow their natural bent. And just as paradoxically, they
were warned that God rewarded the virtuous with success,

pouring His bounty upon the industrious, the frugal, and the clean of mind and body. Presumably, any worthy natural bents then were those that society recognized as deserving of large financial rewards, such as business, and not the more base occupations, such as domestic labor or factory work. Where the Puritans claimed the poor were seldom sinners, but treated them as deficient, the ideologists of the nineteenth century pronounced them to be outright wicked. Success required no explanations beyond the pointing of a finger to the individual hero, while failure permitted no excuses for its sufferers.

During this time, then, egalitarian values lost ground to individualistic ones. Not only was inequality acceptable, it was preferred. Where the Puritan wealthy castigated themselves for being tempted to enjoy their fortunes, the capitalist barons of the 1800s flaunted their pleasures and publicized their lives of opulence and decadence.

Accompanying this conspicuous consumption, however, was the requirement that the public be served as well. Also, since men were to be self-made, it was not considered proper that a magnate should transmit his fortune to his children. Even rich men's sons were to prove their mettle. Consequently, men like Carnegie, Cornell, and Vanderbilt saw that portions of their income went to charities, schools, hospitals, and other social foundations. Nonetheless, they managed in spite of their efforts to leave behind sizeable. holdings, and some of the wealthiest families today owe their position to the wisdom of their ancestors over one hundred years ago.

Of course, the success myth was aimed at a particular segment of the population—to white males, preferably of Anglo-Saxon heritage. Protestants disproportionately acquired mansions in Newport and Saratoga, just as Irish disproportionately dwelt in the servants' coveys of these buildings. Blacks, recent immigrants from Southern and Eastern Europe, and women need not heed the gospel of Horatio Alger fiction. The first two groups were not considered of proper temperament to handle positions of responsibility, and women's calling placed them in the parlor, kitchen, and bedroom. Each of these types was thought biologically unsuited for the industry of business, though suited well enough for sweat shops, mines, or mills.

Each was thought to lack perseverance, except when it came to six-day-a-week, fourteen-hour shifts. While it was all right for striving young men to be of good cheer, mill women who danced little jigs in excitement over a good job were fired. Actions held to be evidence for promotion for one group of the population were considered minimal standards of good work behavior for the rest.

By the start of the twentieth century, the inequalities were fixed. Blacks found work only at the most menial and taxing physical labor, or as tenant farmers on small, unproductive plots of land. Women were to stay home, if "ladies" of the middle class, or strain their backs, eyes, and fingers in piece-work manufacture of clothes and small goods, or more rarely, as secretaries and nurses. Most white males worked in factories, dark offices, or shops. But the rooms of power, whether in stores, banks, or city halls, belonged to persons who shared identical badges of skin color and genitalia. To be a white male augured no guarantee of success, but to be otherwise presaged a certainty of failure.

By 1900, then, in the economic realm the Revolution had failed. Although slaves no longer existed, all men did not have equal access to the fictitious tollways. Black men laboring long hours, performing with all the virtues of the self-made men, earned barely enough to feed their kind. Immigrant men with swarthy faces and tongue-twisting names sweated in factories to support their families in dank tenement rooms. Women were not yet equal citizens in government, let alone thought of as fully mature or productive. That city and farm wives alike sewed their own clothes, baked their bread, canned their food, boiled their soap, and carried their water was ignored in discussions of their "weakness." In light of these realities, the inspirational literature was a mockery.[18]

SELF OVER SOCIETY

Almost a century has passed since the voices of the success preachers exhorted their cause in magazines, newspapers, and books. It would appear the inequalities of early industrialism

too have passed. Women vote, blacks sit where they wish on
buses, and men with Slavic names serve in the state houses.
U.S. citizens enjoy one of the highest overall standards of living
in the world. Even the poorest households have televisions, re-
frigerators, and indoor plumbing. It seems the land of plenty,
the cornucopia that schoolchildren color in at Thanksgiving
and pin on their bulletin boards.

Prophets of success no longer wear clerical collars as in earlier centuries. Werner Erhard, the quintessential self-made
man, tells his followers if they've "got it," they can "get it."[19]
Richard Bolles and others in vocational counselling advise that
with sufficient hard work, determination, and hours of
self-analysis, anyone at all, including women, blacks, poor,
disabled, and aged can get a satisfying and rewarding job.[20]
Self-help books assure that a change in what one wears at the
job or writes in a memo will bring a fatter paycheck and a
larger office. The messages sing a litany in which "Pray for us"
as the basis for grace and salvation in heaven is replaced by
"Change us" as the means to riches on earth.

Not surprisingly, Americans have grown into a sanguine lot
about their fates. In the most detailed and recent study of attitudes toward success, Richard Coleman and Lee Rainwater
found that almost everyone they questioned readily and enthu-
siastically provided stories of success among their friends and
in their own families.[21] The ease and speed of these responses
suggest that discussions of class mobility are part of the essential fabric of everyday conversations in our society. Were Cot-
ton Mather, Benjamin Franklin, or Horatio Alger, Jr. to speak
with these descendants, they would find many places of agreement, yet question the morality of the beliefs.

Like the Puritans, contemporary Americans believe in the
existence of social classes, or the "niches each of us fits into."
They are more sophisticated than their forebears in recognizing
that people are assorted by wealth, job, education, work location, lifestyle, and ethnicity. Of all these measures, most important is money, pure and simple, a notion that would knock
off many old New Englanders' hats.

More akin with Franklin and followers, Americans today
view the class system as fluid in shape, one moving increas-

ingly toward a situation of equality, where most people enjoy a comfortable standard of living. As proof of this, they point to barriers that have fallen in recent years, for example, in the areas of job and educational discrimination. They also argue that prejudices related to ancestry or religion that their grand-parents experienced no longer rule.

They seem to have swallowed Horatio Alger whole. While admitting that social classes exist, they are quick to point out that the higher positions are not out of reach. The situation isn't "a rigid once-you're-born-into-it-you-can't-get-out-of-it sort of thing," they explain. Rather, class distinctions form the ladder for the game called "social climbing." Individual Americans may disagree over the number of steps on the lad-der, but not over its existence or the opportunity to climb.

Through reference to personal knowledge of cases of up-ward mobility, they argue that America is a fluid society in which effort and drive more often than not are rewarded. In the stories they offer of relatives who achieved a good social standing in spite of poor circumstances, the emphasis is that in-dividual action, not inherited social mobility, provided the basis for success. They claim that the most effective ways for a person to improve her or his social standing are parental en-couragement, a good education, and ambition to get ahead. In the public ideal, social mobility is more rule than rarity, pri-marily the result of an individual's perspicacity in recognizing and making opportunities. Education and parental encourage-ment direct the action toward success, but work ("pure effort," "sheer work," "perseverance") and ambition ("drive," "deter-mination," "desire") provide the main thrust.

The notion of "calling" has disappeared from these tales. So, too, has any sense that those in better positions have a respon-sibility to the community. Those with money can enjoy it, and magazines such as *People* or *Us* provide readers with vicarious pleasure of riches, models of hope, and (for the less advan-taged) sources of frustration. While some family dynasties continue to practice *noblesse oblige* and fund cultural or social institutions, the popular heroes and heroines of sports, popular media, and business rarely express such social conscience. The robber barons would be disgusted by such uninterest.

One curious religious-moral remnant from the past pervades our attitudes toward the poor. While the rich may not be thought of as saved or saintly, the poor are certainly damned and sinful. Downward mobility is punishment for social dereliction. When asked to discuss cases of status loss, Americans from all levels of society are likely to point to alcohol as the devil's worker. Many have friends who "threw away all their advantages by drinking to the point where they couldn't keep a job." Other common faults are "laziness," a "don't-care attitude," "unwillingness to work at anything," and other character faults. Accordingly, if a woman falls below her class of birth, it is held she married badly, that is, to a man who drinks, gets into trouble, or lacks ambition. The only circumstance in which a loss in status is viewed sympathetically is when it occurs as the result of a traumatic, disabling disease or a mental illness. Otherwise, the verdict is that a person should have the strength to "get through tough situations."

Not surprisingly, Americans prefer to cast themselves among the select—almost all claim that they have moved up significantly within their own social class or to the class above that of their parents. They point to cars, furniture, and other property as proof. In fact, such claims represent distortion and selective perception. As will be seen in detail later, the chances for significant upward mobility in our society are not that great for many people, and the possibility of downward mobility definitely does exist. Although class *consciousness* may be waning in our society, the class *order* persists.

Coleman and Rainwater suggest that the current American Dream represents an *effortocracy*, in which ambition, energy, and application are believed to be the rewarded virtues. The illusion of self-choice reigns. This contrasts with another view, more common among intellectuals and policy makers, that the dream represents a *meritocracy*, in which talent and quality are thought to earn power and wealth. The point over which average Americans and those espousing meritocracy disagree is the distribution of ability. The former imply that most jobs can be done by most people, and perhaps would even agree with their nineteenth-century kin that genius can be more of a liability than an asset in a worker.

Contemporary Americans accept as many paradoxes in their thinking as did their Puritan forefathers. They are qualified egalitarians who want people fed and well-clothed, though not through handouts. They prefer that the poor be given many options to earn their own meals and winter coats, for only morally irresponsible persons would wish it otherwise. This was evident during the civil rights and poverty movements of the sixties, when social policies placed money in self-help programs rather than direct income grants. At the same time, they do not want so much equality that competition disappears. Each wants the chance, however small, to strike it rich, and to enjoy exclusively the benefits of wealth that have been deservedly earned by one's self and family, and are hence not to be shared with the less fortunate.

One of the last questions Coleman and Rainwater asked their respondents was, "What sort of changes in social class in America would you like to see in the future, and why these?" This provoked the most explosive answers of any to their survey. On one extreme, interviewers heard, "Social class is the dirtiest thing I ever heard of!"; at the other, "It's a challenge to any red-blooded American!" Overall, most people were accepting of the system, and only a minority could conceive of a classless society. Most acknowledged the hierarchy and competition, though for varying reasons. Like the Puritans, some called it the "law of life." Others wanted the game of social mobility to continue, with modifications in the rules concerning restrictions on race, religion, or ancestry. Still others accepted class differences, so long as those at the bottom did not live in poverty. Throughout these explanations, the effortocratic ideal reigned, as summed up by one Kansas respondent, "No one should get a free ride through life."

THE FINAL CORRUPTION

In its early days the Dream served as a necessary incentive for a diverse population that had to meet its survival needs or die. There was no room for narcissism on the frontier. As the country matured, the Dream expanded, promising people more for their efforts and demanding more of them. As the society became more urban and industrialized, it provided workers with strong motivation while urging them to behave in ways well suited for large, hierarchical work places.

Until the twentieth century, the success myths spun a complex web of egalitarian ideals, social welfare, and individualism. The self-made man was a member of a community and owed it to others to behave with honor, decency, and compassion. Although most men became neither clear successes nor out-and-out failures, they could be satisfied with themselves for living a virtuous life.

The contemporary American Dream has lost this moral base and turned into a ghostly caricature of itself. It urges that people should persevere, plan, analyze, and ultimately reshape themselves, the better to acquire wealth and power. The ego is the center of activity, existing autonomously in the world with no responsibilities to others outside one's family and intimates (and even these ties are tenuous). Franklin has been turned on his head—one had better express some dishonesty and deceit in dealing with others, because they only expect such chicanery.

Thus, the American Dream acknowledges that the well-off and the powerful are not necessarily to be admired, since wealth may come from other than laudable means. This matters little, however, for respect and honor are no longer important goals in life—to be rich enough to indulge hedonistic pursuits is sufficient. Americans will gladly play dice with the devil and chance virtue for comfort. As if the material deprivations of poverty were not enough, our social service institutions provide their pittances in exchange for the humiliation and degradation of their needy clients.

Simply put, the American Dream molds both the private inner worlds of Americans and their relations with others in a way that conflicts with the values of egalitarianism and social welfare. Much of the current tension in our society concerning equal rights reflects these contradictions. In offering an interpretation of reality that is fallacious, it inspires false hopes, needless self-blame, and unjust anger toward others. Most curiously, in the social realm it pervades all political viewpoints, from conservative to radical. Any recommendation concerning the alleviation of inequality will be undermined by its false premises.

In recent years, the dramatic conflict over inequalities has centered upon affirmative action. Allan Bakke's case against the Medical School at the University of California and Brian Weber's suit against Kaiser Aluminum are only two of hundreds of claims fought in the courts in the past decade. The high unemployment and inflation of the seventies have left people haggling over the division of scarcer, expensive goods. Some of the most outspoken liberal spokespeople and social critics of the sixties are arguing for a "New Conservatism" and the dismantling of antidiscrimination regulations. Minority groups and women's support groups are dismayed by what they see as meager progress. The strength of the backlash against them has provoked confusion and a lack of well-articulated goals. Bitterness and hopelessness sound from activists and traditionalists alike.

The debates are sidetracked by facile labelling of issues— black versus white, women versus men, liberals versus conservatives—as though teams were in competition. This definition of the situation itself reflects the American dream with its requirement that there be clear winners and losers. What is overlooked is the fact that these various groups, however different their stated interest, are grounded upon a shared culture, and that the source of disagreement reflects fissures and faults in that culture. The problem is not that they disagree over the direction the country should take, so much as they are all loyal Americans, devoted to an image of social order that is even more inaccurate than the Puritan's cosmology or Poor Richard's precepts. Unless the myth itself is attacked directly, the resolutions of disputes among the interest groups can only be temporary or superficial. Otherwise, its distorted veneration of narcissism, competition, and hierarchy will continue to corrode what bases for social equality remain in our society.

Chapter 2

One Man's Dream

To get beyond racism, we must first take account of race. And to treat some persons equally, we must treat them differently.
                    Supreme Court Justice Harry A. Blackmun

The guarantee of equal protection cannot mean one thing when applied to one individual and something else when applied to a person of another color.
                    Supreme Court Justice Lewis F. Powell

In late 1973, a pleasant-looking, athletic, blond man of 32 sat in his ranch house in Los Altos, California, filling out a form.[1] Little could he guess that six years later his photograph would appear on the front page of the *New York Times*, that in living rooms and bars across the country his name would be spoken—by some respectfully, admiringly, by others disparagingly. By the very private act of applying to medical school, Allan Bakke, a seclusive and retiring person, unintentionally ensured that he would become the major symbol in the seventies of economic inequality.

In his mind was the simple determination to change careers, to leave a lucrative position in aeronautics research for four years of medical school, followed by several more of internship and residency. He did not act impulsively; he had been working toward this opportunity for almost a decade. He was a man with a dream, a man undeterred.

When Allan Bakke was growing up, he probably gave little thought to becoming a doctor. His father delivered mail; his mother taught school. A brilliant student, he did not have the financial resources to attend a top private college. In the fifties, wealth and connections still mattered strongly in entry to such schools, and scholarships for mail carriers' sons were few. So Bakke did what most youths in similar circumstances did—he attended a public institution, the University of Minnesota. By majoring in engineering, he could enter a profession which did not require postgraduate studies for the achievement of a good position.

To support his education, he enrolled in a Naval Reserve Officers Training Corps Program. Thus, upon graduating with an A average, he faced four years of debt to the military. To satisfy this requirement, he joined the Marines. It was during this duty, particularly while in Vietnam, that he observed closely the work of physicians and decided that his interests rested in medicine and serving people, not in engineering and serving machines.

Once discharged, he took a job as an aeronautics engineer with NASA's Ames Research Center in Palo Alto. But after hours he took courses at local colleges to cover the requirements for a pre-med degree. More unusual, and proof of his commitment, he became a volunteer at a local hospital, a role usually filled by women in candy-striped smocks. Ten years after his college graduation, he finally had the resources and course requirements to make the try for medical school. Applying to eleven schools, he asked that they take into consideration the reasons for his rather late start. In spite of his exceptional record of aptitude test scores, grade averages, and evidence of dedication, all eleven rejected him.

INVISIBLE BARRIERS

Unfortunately, Allan Bakke was caught in a net of historical changes he could not have anticipated. Had he applied to medical school right after college, in 1962, his record would undoubtedly have earned him entry.[2] Of course, to have done so, he would have needed the means to support his endeavor, and it was that lack of means that had misdirected him to engineering in the first place. In 1972 he was hampered by unfavorable shifts in population dynamics and cultural changes, which both increased competition for entrance to medical school and modified the criteria for the selection of students.

In 1962, Bakke was competing with those his own age, chil-

dren of the early years of World War II, when the birthrate had
been low. In 1972 he joined those of the fifties' baby boom.
Along with the increase in number of competitors, the rules of
medical school admission narrowed. In 1968, blacks, who
composed about 12 percent of the general population, filled
less than 3 percent of entering medical spaces; by 1970 this figure doubled.[3] These increases reflect schools' successful attempts to be more sensitive to minority needs. Naturally, during this period the proportion of spaces held by whites
dropped. So when Bakke received his rejection letter, he was
among 22,000 other disappointed aspirants around the country.
In fact, only one out of three applicants made it to *any* medical
school that year,[4] and the chances of acceptance by Davis were
24 to 1.[5]

In its short history, the Davis faculty realized, it had copied
other schools and adopted racially-exclusive patterns. Its entering class of 1968 had only three minorities, all Asian, out of
fifty students, while the minority population in California overall was 25 percent. Pressure from civil rights groups and federal
regulations, as well as social altruism, spurred the faculty to
form a special committee to develop a more heterogeneous
student body.

This group readily identified subtle racist bias in its admission procedures. For example, they discovered that on the two
commonest criteria for acceptance, the college grade point average (GPA) and the Medical Concepts Aptitude Test (MCAT),
all nonwhite groups, except Asians, scored lower overall, for
reasons relating to their low status in society. These students
have less adequate preparation for college, hence must devote
college time to learning skills advantaged students bring with
them. Being more likely to work full-time as students, they
lack the leisure to explore course interests as fully as they
would like. Since low incomes force them to take longer to
complete school, they often marry and take on family responsibility before they graduate. Finally, more have had linguistic
and cultural experiences different from those tested in the
MCAT. In other words, minority students are handicapped in
the competition by years of unfair treatment and because the
contest fails to include tests in those areas where minorities are

strong. Minority supporters thus argued that while the disadvantaged students may have slightly lower test scores and grades, they had proven the ambition and determination demanded by the medical profession.[6]

GPAs and MCATs do not measure many traits believed to be needed for proficient doctoring—intuition, interpersonal sensitivity, empathy, ability to communicate with people of various ages and backgrounds, and so on. (Many of us have encountered a doctor with obviously superior technical skills, but lacking any interest in or understanding of us as individual personalities.) In fact, neither score even predicts medical school success well.[7] In other words, two students with identical scores may end up in very different positions on class ranking by graduation day, and display widely divergent clinical ability. For this reason, schools have not used grades or test scores as the only or major criteria for accepting students. Admissions committees look at personality, community and campus activities, work history, personal history, and aspirations within medicine, among others.

In light of this knowledge, the Davis task force recommended that a special program be instituted to admit disadvantaged students. Under this plan a number of slots would be reserved for consideration by a Special Admissions Committee composed primarily of minority medical faculty and students. The committee was to begin its selection with the same information as the regular admissions committee, but it would not invoke the same requirements. Rather, it was to locate students who had been genuinely disadvantaged in terms of means, poor education, the need to work through school, and such, and accept them in spite of GPA or MCAT scores that were lower than those admitted through the regular process. In 1970, eight students entered under this program, and the Davis faculty found their performance satisfying enough to expand the size of this group.

When Allan Bakke applied in 1972, the committee had set aside 16 of 100 slots for special admissions. Had he submitted his forms early in the fall as he had originally hoped to do, he might well have been admitted, for that was when most of the class was selected. Unfortunately, his mother-in-law was dying of lung cancer, and he chose to join his family in Iowa to support and care for her. In the midst of this personal tragedy, he delayed completing his application until January. By then only a few regular positions remained open.

Aware of the special admissions program, Allan Bakke felt aggrieved. He wondered why students with lower grades and test scores had been given special treatment. His engineer's glasses doubtless shaped his perception of the admissions process. To him, the numbers on his test scores were higher, hence he was better qualified. In this society, the best person wins, and in our computer-based world, the measure of winning is more often than not a number. Nice guys don't win ball games—it's the ones who hit the most home runs.

Nowhere can one find evidence of explicit racism in his reaction.[8] Nevertheless, it is the nature of bigotry in our society that without awareness white people act in discriminatory ways and demean nonwhites for their color alone. Allan Bakke's past prepared him well in this regard. He grew up in a country where residential segregation prevented him as a white from confronting the errors in the stereotypes about minorities perpetrated by the media and in daily conversations. Such isolation precluded him from appreciating the daily insults of living in substandard housing; of attending old, crowded, and poorly equipped schools; of being policed by people from outside the neighborhood or culture; of being ignored by city agencies which clean streets, collect garbage, and maintain parks; and of experiencing a hundred similar indignities that visit upon people trapped and defined by the impoverished area they live in.

As a university student in Minnesota, a state with relatively few minorities, and as an officer in the Marines, he could not have the kinds of experiences with nonwhites that would acquaint him with the facts of pervasive racial discrimination in our society. Certainly he was very unlikely to have met blacks in his work, for engineering is one of the whitest of all occupations.

Allan Bakke had been systematically denied an appreciation of the facts of disadvantage in our society as it especially affects minorities. He was an ignorant man—oblivious to the lawful legacy unleashed by two centuries of slavery and discrimination, protected by the preserve of his white skin from comprehending the carefully choreographed denial of educational, economic, and housing resources inflicted upon nonwhites.

The case was much simpler, as far as he was concerned. That nonwhites were given a special admissions program at Davis meant he was being denied equal treatment solely by reason of his race. He would not accept that his age had anything to do with it, nor any of the other qualifications taken into account by the admissions committee, such as his ability to empathize and communicate with patients. Following his rejection, he communicated some of these thoughts in a letter to the admissions committee chairperson.

At this point the letter was passed on to another member for response. It happened to be a person who considered himself "stubbornly fair-minded," and who was distressed that able nonminority candidates were being hurt by the Special Admissions Program. Dr. Peter Storandt expressed his support of Bakke, assured him of his talent, and in time dropped the seed of the basis for a lawsuit. The two men eventually met in person to discuss litigation strategies.[9]

To set up his case as strongly as possible, Bakke made one more try at admission to the program by placing on file a strong dossier. There he stated, "I have an excellent job in engineering and am well-paid. I don't wish to change careers for financial gain, but because I truly believe my contribution to society can be much greater as a physician-engineer than in my present field. I'm not afraid of hard work, I enjoy and have been successful at working with others, and know my motivation is as strong and honest toward a career of service in medicine as that of any applicant."[10] Here was a faithful son of American society, appealing to the fathers that he had the virtues for achievement—the hard work and motivation to back up his established ability. No wonder Bakke was eventually frustrated; he was just the type of exemplary figure that the culture promised him should expect the attainment of the American Dream.

As a thoroughly enculturated member of society, Allan Bakke did not have the objectivity to see the problems and contradictions inherent in the American success ideology.

Ironically, it was his very naive acceptance of American ideals that led him to force their enactment. Had he been more aware of the paradoxes of success and inequality in our society, he might have become too cynical to think he could ever reach his goal.

When Bakke hired an attorney, his primary goal was simply to find a place to study medicine. His lawyer negotiated with Davis: "Just find another cadaver for him and there'll be no need for a suit."[11] The school gave serious consideration to the possibility, but thought it would set a dangerous precedent for irregular admissions. Bakke's personal quest became tied to larger social policy only after all other channels had failed. His lawyer took up the issue of unequal treatment and argued it successfully before the California Supreme Court. In deciding in favor of Bakke, the justices noted: "The lofty purpose of the equal protection clause of the Fourteenth Amendment is incompatible with the premise that some races may be afforded a higher degree of protection against unequal treatment than others." The Fourteenth Amendment avows:

> No state shall make or enforce any law which shall abridge the privileges or immunities of citizens of the United States, nor shall any State deprive any person of life, liberty, or property, without due process of law; nor deny to any person within its jurisdiction the equal protection of the laws.

During the sixties, this principle had been the keystone for civil rights cases. Now, ironically, a white person was invoking the same amendment to gain equal protection.

DIVISION AND DEBATE

The University of California could have chosen simply to admit Bakke and revamp its admission procedures accordingly. Instead, it took the case to the United States Supreme Court. Whether this represented a moral stand on the school's part is debatable. The University of California is on record for its failure to hire and promote accomplished women and minority staff. It has fewer minority students than the state college and

university system, a separate body of state schools that are neither as well-funded nor as richly staffed.

Indeed, other facts suggest that the school filed the appeal
with some hopes that the concept of affirmative action would
be overturned. The case was so weak that some civil rights advocates attempted to persuade university administrators to
withdraw their plan. Critics observed correctly that few affirmative admissions programs around the country were as exclusive as that at Davis. Also, the school had changed its admissions forms in a way difficult to defend on the grounds of
the Fourteenth Amendment. Whereas in 1973 it asked applicants if they wished to be considered as from an educationally
or economically deprived background, and to explain why, in
1974 it requested simply that they state their race. So clearly a
racially-based exclusion was operating.

Furthermore, the school did not prepare its case well. The
best that can be said for the university counsel's legal efforts is
that they were lackadaisacal.[12] It agreed with Bakke's counsel
to have the case tried without oral testimony. This left the evidence to be presented by briefs, and in reading the two sides it
does not take long to see that Bakke's lawyers were more dili-
gent and perceptive in forming their arguments. The university
neglected to address important details of the Davis plan—even
why it had been thought necessary by faculty. It did not address Bakke's repeated assertion that he was better qualified in
terms of test results than admitted minority students, and in
doing so, implicitly encouraged the view that only numerical
scores mattered in admissions decisions. It failed to document
the extensive history of discrimination within the state and university. And more curiously, it neglected mention of a dean's
special admissions program, under which white children of politically well-connected University supporters or contributors
had been admitted to the medical school in spite of qualifications clearly below those submitted by Bakke.[13] Filing the appeal was a convenient way for the university to acquire the
aura of being a socially committed institution when in fact,
considering its treatment of disadvantaged employees and students, this was patently false.

In ignoring the subtleties of the case, the media provoked

hasty public polarization. In California, the reactions were immediate. Several thousand people gathered in San Francisco's Civic Center Plaza to protest the State Court's actions. A National Committee to Overturn the Bakke Decision formed, which stimulated the participation of groups interested in asserting the priority of affirmative actions over others rights. Groups supportive of Bakke quickly garnered financial resources to publicize their side.

Radicals concluded that Bakke was a racist white, and failed to consider his unprivileged background, one that had denied him access to medical school in his early years. Conservatives viewed the University of California as an institution that was out to sacrifice academic quality for the sake of social retributions. Neither plaintiff nor defendant was so purely drawn as the extremists presumed.

Only the Supreme Court briefs themselves disclose the complexity of the matter. The full document runs over 3,500 pages long, of which a small portion consists of statements by the counsels on behalf of the university and Bakke. Over forty sponsors introduced *amicus* briefs, a procedure whereby those with a special interest in a case can file their reasons for supporting a particular side. Predictably, the NAACP, NOW, the Urban League, and the Farm Workers supported the university, while the Fraternal Order of Police and the Young Americans for Freedom championed Bakke. Yet some groups taking opposing sides had been bedfellows during earlier days of civil rights, and curious crossovers occurred. Staid universities with poor records in affirmative action rallied behind California. The conservative National Education Association aligned with the university as well, while the more liberal and activist American Federation of Teachers joined with Bakke. Organizations of Jewish sponsorship that had supported minority groups in the past now sided with the fairhaired man.

That Bakke was backed by some traditionally liberal groups, and the university by some conservative ones, reflects the dilemmas this country faces in ensuring equal rights and opportunities. Liberal Jews, among the first to support black rights with their voices and pocketbooks, looked into their own history and saw in the Davis program a variation of racial quotas that have been and continue to be used to exclude them from full participation in social life. They argued that the emphasis upon statistical integration was making the public more aware of racial and ethnic differences, hence exacerbating the possibility for the acceptance of individuals apart from their background. Liberal groups such as the American Federation of Teachers also worried that individual merit as a basis for awarding success was being eroded. The elite universities, while speaking a social welfare rhetoric, may have been using this opportunity to suggest to their major source of research funds, the federal government, that they were behind equal opportunity.

Scarcely any of the Bakke supporters argued in racist terms. Only two briefs presented inflammatory, racially derogatory claims. These were entered by a group of college professors and administrators, names once known for being in the liberal vanguard, such as Bruno Bettleheim, Nathan Glazer, Sidney Hook, Walter Rostow, and Oscar Handlin. In giving their reason for filing a brief, they claimed that reverse discrimination was "rampant throughout the United States," in undergraduate, graduate, and professional schools, both in student admissions and faculty personnel policies. The clear implication was that white males were "being cruelly denied their rights to self-fulfillment and meaningful careers." To put black students in medical schools could only inflict a "trauma" of eventual "shame and humiliation."[14]

For the most part the Bakke supporters offered carefully reasoned positions, as did the briefs in favor of the university. Taken together, the two sides offered a dramatic enactment of conflicts in values and attitudes that threaten to rift our society from time to time. Where the Bakke side stressed the rights of individuals, the university side emphasized social good, insisting that the time for reparations to minorities was at hand, that the nation could ill afford the loss of their talent. Where Bakke supporters argued the principle of merit, preferably as based upon numerical grades and tests, the university advocates pointed to the unreliability of such measures as the sole predictors of performance in so complex a job as medicine. Where the Bakke briefs claimed that reverse discrimination was punishing worthy males, the university documents reminded of the pervasive and persistent discrimination against minorities in our society.

Doing disservice to both sides, the media misrepresented the case. "Reverse discrimination" was now used in newscasts where once one had heard "affirmative action." One read of "racial quotas" as though all the country were now parcelled into statistical divisions. Visions of illiterate dark-skinned healers hovered between the lines. Few writers noted the irony in the fact that civil rights groups were arguing with each other. Commentators exaggerated the import of the Court decision by suggesting that in a stroke of its members' signatures, the cause of economic equality for minorities could be completely defeated or firmly established.

RESOLUTION AND CONFUSION

When the nine judges appeared before the public on June 28, 1978, they proffered a Solomonic compromise, in which, through a complicated series of split decisions, they allowed partial satisfaction to both parties in the dispute. First, they decided that the Davis system, one based upon a clear-cut numerical quota, was not an acceptable procedure. As Justice Powell wrote, "It is evident that the Davis special admission program involves the use of an explicit racial classification never before countenanced by this Court. It tells applicants who are not Negro, Asian, or 'Chicano' that they are totally excluded from a specific percentage of seats in an entering class. No matter how strong their qualifications, quantitative and extracurricular, including their own potential for contribution to educational diversity, they are never afforded the chance to compete with applicants from the preferred groups for the special admissions seats." Consequently, the Davis program violated the civil rights guaranteed by the Fourteenth Amendment, and Bakke as a consequence was to be admitted to the medical school. (Since this was not a class action case,

only Allan Bakke was directly affected by this decision.) Thus a
slim majority of the Court upheld the general principle of individualism.

Yet at the same time the Court affirmed the right of schools
to take race into account during admissions, just as they have
traditionally included social background, leadership skills,
special talents, the applicant's home region, and such. It made
reference to the procedures followed by Harvard College as
one acceptable model. "When the committee on admissions
reviews the large middle groups of applicants who are 'admis-
sible' and deemed capable of doing good work in their courses,
the race of an applicant may tip the balance in his favor, just as
geographic origin or a life spent on a farm may tip the balance
in other candidates' cases. A farm boy from Idaho can bring
something to Harvard College that a Bostonian cannot offer.
Similarly, a black student can usually bring something that a
white person cannot offer." In such cases, though all races
compete with each other, to be nonwhite may be considered a
"plus" on the applicant's behalf. The Court further mentioned
its decisions on school desegregation, economic discrimination,
and gender discrimination as reminders of its commitment to
the elimination of inequalities.

Though this summary fairly states the specific decisions
handed down by the Court, it fails to catch the contradictory
flavor of the justices' separate arguments. In fact, early news
stories said simply "Bakke Wins" because wire service personnel had had so much difficulty making sense of the Justice's responses. They had split five to four on each of the three issues:
admitting Bakke, invalidating the quota system at Davis, af-
firming the use of race in admissions programs. In fact, six of
the nine justices wrote separate opinions, which, taken together, repeat the adversarial nature of the briefs. For example,
Justice Brennan claimed that whites as a class are "not saddled
with such disabilities, or subjected to such a history of purposeful unequal treatment, or relegated to such a position of
political powerlessness" as minority groups. But Justice Powell
wrote, "The white 'majority' itself is composed of various minority groups, most of which can lay claim to a history of prior

discrimination at the hands of the state and private individuals." No wonder the journalists were confused!

That the Bakke case provided little basis for resolution of these debates is a testimony to the American system of adjudication. The confusions and contradictions of the Court mirrored the mood of the citizenry. The case itself was not as important in the legal history of the civil rights movement as the media inferred it to be. It affected directly the admission of one person, and stimulated universities and professional schools to revise their entry procedures. Nonetheless, the case revitalized and inflamed old arguments within the society at large, and served to keep civil rights issues before the public consciousness.

The combatants in the Bakke case—liberals and conservatives, unionists and free enterprisers, nonwhites and ethnics—all agreed on one point: Allan Bakke had a right to dream and to pursue his hopes in reality. As a mail carrier's son he could aspire to one of the most prestigious jobs in the country. The debate was over the nature of the competition for that job, whether Bakke was being treated as fairly as the black daughter of an Oakland dry cleaner or the young man from a Los Angeles barrio. In other words, the dispute was characteristically American.

The American Federation of Teachers summed up the issue succinctly: "This country was founded upon the proposition that it is the worth of the individual that was paramount. We are not a country of castes and discreet classes. We are a nation of individuals, each of whom is to be judged upon his own merit, not his class or background."[15] The Bakke supporters interpreted this to mean that the test of merit must be the same for all. The University supporters argued that individuals from disadvantaged backgrounds must be judged both on their merit and their personal history. To both sides an individual's right to success was unquestioned.

Missing from the dispute was any recognition that the starting assumption itself, the American Dream, was at the base of the conflict. No one asked why so few jobs in medicine and other fields are ripe plums in our society. No one wondered

whether the competitive process was really the best way to locate compassionate healers. No one considered the artificial
limits imposed by the medical professions on the supply of
doctors. No one suggested that the rewards for doctoring be
leveled, or those for other health care work, such as nursing, be
increased.

The game was fixed, and everyone seemed satisfied with its
outcome. All in all, the efforts and arguments behind the Bakke
case were over a minor rule change. Richly symbolic, the event
made little difference in the country's move toward a system of
equality.

Chapter 3

The Myth
of Reverse
Discrimination

We have civil-righted so hard that now you are discriminating against me.

White union worker

Black is when folks say you've got to earn the rights the Constitution guaranteed you already had.

Turner Brown, Jr., Black Is

The Bakke decision could not help but complicate an increasingly perplexing situation, for the mood of the country in regard to opportunity was less secure in 1978 than it had been several years earlier. Civil rights activities had mushroomed during a time when the economy was swelling temporarily in response to war. If ever there seemed a moment when minorities might receive their just due with little threat to others, this was it. Then the economy moved into a period of persistent inflation, high unemployment, and a capricious labor market, one in which even highly trained people were finding themselves to be unemployable. In such eras of little slack, people defensively pull back their support for policies aimed at eliminating economic inequality. In the more fluid and affluent era of the sixties, whites could agree that the disadvantaged deserved more positions and promotions, for opportunities were opening up for everyone. But by the late seventies, the competition had tightened, and those who had been accustomed to holding a privileged position in the contest for good jobs and pay grew less inclined to give up that advantage.

This growing conservatism showed up in attitude surveys.[1] For example, in 1978, whites believed that on the whole racial discrimination at work was a thing of the past. However, even more blacks than a decade earlier felt that they were missing out on jobs and promotions because of their race. Clearly, two conflicting views of reality were operating here.

From the perspective of mass media the optimism of the conservatives reigned. "You've come a long way, baby!" So a 1970 cigarette advertisement slogan now reminded the readers of a woman's magazine. Baseball teams, lily-white thirty years earlier, now sported a palette of brown faces from cream to ebony. Women sat in the presidential cabinet, and a black man sat on the Supreme Court. Nightly newscasts deemed it eventful to interview women who had broken into new roles—as telephone linepersons, as space-shuttle trainees, as executives of corporations. Television fiction portrayed working women—single or divorced mothers—and families of blacks whose members worked at mainline jobs. Government statisticians told us that more women were working than ever and that black family income was rapidly rising. Yes, it would seem we'd come a long way as a country in fulfilling the American Dream.

But had we? Were women and people of color finding the equality of opportunity they had so loudly demonstrated for and marched for and gone to jail for during the sixties?

According to some, not only was equality here, but previously disadvantaged people were getting the gain on the once-privileged. They claimed there was now "reverse discrimination," a policy that prevented white males from getting their equal due. Those holding these attitudes would have us leave well enough alone, for equal opportunity, if not quite available to every person in every life arena, is clearly around the corner. To offer special advantages to women and blacks would be to discriminate against white men on the basis of their sex and race. This view, we have seen, was the essence of the Bakke case.

Proponents of these ideas were of all political persuasions. They included liberal administrators of Ivy League universities, conservative meat packers in the Midwest, moderate school teachers on the West Coast, and radical union organizers in the South. They included women and members of racial minorities as well. They confessed their fears in conversations with friends and in letters to editors of both mass media and specialized magazines.

In clear opposition were those who agreed with Justice Marshall's comments on the Bakke case: "Measured by any benchmark of conduct of achievement, meaningful equality remains a distant dream for the Negro. It is because of a legacy of unequal treatment that we now must permit the institutions of this society to give consideration to race in making decisions about who will hold the positions of influence, affluence, and prestige in America. If we are ever to become a fully integrated society, one in which the color of a person's skin will not determine the opportunities available to him or her, we must be willing to take the steps to open those doors."[2] People sympathetic with Marshall's statement added other persons who have suffered as well—women, other racial minorities, and religious or cultural minorities. Thus the writing of feminists and spokespersons for racial activism repeated the same messages first broadcast in the sixties: that many people in our society continue to be disadvantaged because of some physical appearance or language style or telltale last name.

This debate, as to whether or not once-oppressed groups are getting their due, is the first test of the American Dream. If in fact inequality is waning, then we can turn our scarce resources toward our other problems. And if, as Bakke (and similar lawsuits) implied, white males are now receiving unfair treatment in the achievement game, then certainly our social policies should be reconsidered. But if equality is not increasing, then we have many questions to ask of the success myth, and are impelled to address the failure of current equal opportunity policies.

THE DREAM PUT TO THE TEST

According to the Constitution, Americans are guaranteed "life, liberty, and the pursuit of happiness." After spending many thousands of dollars on research, some investigators at the University of Chicago proved that to have health, opportunity, and happiness, it helps to have money.[3] The notion of the happy-go-lucky poor is a sweet fantasy spun to soothe the guilt of those in better straits. Thus, for many of the less privileged in our country, the major thrust for the elimination of discrimination should be in the area of economics. To put it bluntly, they want to know who's "getting the action."

Statistics pouring out from government computers suggest that many people are less disadvantaged than they were a few decades ago.[4] For example, in 1940, two-thirds of the nation's blacks lived in rural areas where job and income opportunities were limited. Now, over 70 percent live in metropolitan areas, closer to the industries and office buildings that provide good jobs.

The educational attainment of nonwhites is catching up to that of whites. Currently, about 86 percent of young whites and 76 percent of young blacks have completed high school. For three minorities—Japanese, Chinese, and Filipino—the youngsters have a higher rate of college graduation than whites. The educational attainment of all females, particularly at the college level, is rapidly matching that of men.

Attitudes toward minorities and women, though still prejudicial, are less profound and insidious than in the past. Currently, a considerable plurality of Americans believe blacks are as intelligent and educable as whites (80 percent), would not be disturbed if a black family moved on their block (84 percent), believe children of different races should attend the same school (84 percent). Similarly, respondents to surveys have expressed increasing approval of women working and having careers, even if they are married, and have supported a variety of issues on the feminist docket.[5]

Since 1964, legal changes to encourage equality have forged a strong federal regulatory structure. The Civil Rights Act of 1964 forbade discrimination in all areas of employment, from hiring to firing, and executive orders 11245 and 11375 required that government contractors demonstrate a strong affirmative action policy. As a result of complaints to the Equal Employment Opportunity Commission, such diverse employers as AT&T, Bank of America, and Brown University have been required to show better faith in the hiring of less privileged persons, actively encourage and train such persons, and compensate employees or job applicants who have suffered wage loss or lack of opportunity for promotion as a result of discriminatory practices.

Given these changes in educational opportunity, public attitudes, and laws, it seems logical that economic inequality in our society should also have decreased. Since women and blacks are better educated, we might expect them to find better jobs and earn more than several decades ago. Since prejudice in the population is decreasing, we might expect higher work rates among minorities. Since the 1964 Federal regulations prohibit and punish employer discriminatory practices, we would predict some signs of improvement in all economic measures since that date.

To test these hypotheses, we can examine a number of statistics commonly collected by government and social science researchers:

1. The unemployment rate, which tells how many persons from a group are actively seeking work.
2. Occupational assignment, which tells who is getting what kinds of jobs.
3. Occupational segregation, which describes to what extent people work with their own kind.
4. Occupational prestige, which indicates the desirability of the jobs a group holds.
5. Median earnings for workers over a year.

The best way to study these indicators for our purposes is to see what changes have occurred from the fifties to today, as these trends will show whether civil rights activity has reduced inequality.[6]

Unemployment

The existence of a large number of able and willing potential workers without jobs was a persistent problem during the seventies. Because of affirmative action programs, which require fairness in hiring, we should expect these high rates to be spread evenly across racial, ethnic, and sex groupings in the population. We find the contrary:

- White males are consistently the least likely to be without a job, whatever the year.[7]
- The unemployment gap between whites and blacks, Puerto Ricans, and Mexican Americans has increased in recent years. During the late sixties, a time of economic expansion, the gap appeared to decrease slightly, but virtually all gains were wiped out in the seventies.
- Women are consistently more likely to be unemployed than men of the same race or background.
- The teenage rates are the most dismaying, for it is at this age that crucial job choices are made. In 1978, about 4 of every 10 black youths between 16 and 19 were unemployed, compared to 1 of 10 whites. The prospects for these young women and men seem stark indeed. How will they be able to get jobs in their early twenties if they have several years out of school with little or no work experience?
- Only three minorities studied—the Chinese, Japanese, and Filipino—were not more prone to unemployment than whites.

Thus, going by unemployment data, evidence for discrimination by race and sex is clear. To be black or Hispanic and searching for a job is to be at a considerable disadvantage—the rates average twice that of whites. To be female is also a liability. These patterns have persisted through both fat and lean periods in recent years, which suggests that the unemployment situation for disadvantaged groups is not to be solved by economic measures alone. White men are first hired and last fired in spite of manipulations of the economy to give others a better break. It hasn't come to many of the people who want steady, daylong work.

Occupational Assignment

The reverse discrimination view suggests that disadvantaged people are not just taking jobs from white men—they're taking the better jobs. If this were true, then the proportion of white males in managerial or crafts jobs should have dropped in recent years, to be replaced by more women and minorities. This has not happened.

In 1960, one out of seven white men was a manager or proprietor; this proportion held in the late 1970s. During that time scarcely any other workers moved into that category. Today, one of seventeen white women is a manager, compared to one of twenty black men, and one of thirty-three black women. These figures suggest little threat to the men in the executive suite.

One out of five white men is in skilled crafts, a proportion that has increased slightly since 1960. In contrast, only about one of one hundred women, regardless of race, is working in the trades and on construction sites. However, black men have found a few more doors opening in this area: currently one in six holds a skilled blue-collar job.

Taking all occupations in mind, white men hold the same or better jobs than they did prior to the civil rights legislation. The small gains by other workers came as a result of growth in the economy, not from job-stealing. Where then are all the women who have joined the labor force in recent years? In offices and service establishments, the pink collar ghetto. More women are working because more women's jobs have been created, not because they have pushed into men's work. (The only loss has been for those in need of maids—black women have traded in the kerchief and dust rag of domestic work for the typewriter.)

Occupational Segregation

Were there economic equality, then workers at every level would reflect the rich diversity of people who comprise our nation. Janitors and senators alike would include women, men, blacks, whites, Hispanics, Asians, people with disabilities, and those of diverse cultural orientations. As a way of summarizing to what extent people are integrated at work, social scientists have devised a measure called "occupational segregation," which tells what percent of workers would have to change jobs to distribute work more equitably in our society.

In a society with full work integration, no proportion of workers would have to switch. In the United States, at least 65 percent of all men and women would have to change jobs to equalize assignments by sex, and 38 percent of whites and blacks would have to move to equalize jobs by race.[8] In fact, the amount of job segregation has been increasing since 1960, primarily because Puerto Ricans, Japanese, Filipinos, and Mexican-Americans have been pushed in greater numbers into jobs where their work buddies are unlikely to be white. Only black and Native American males are finding a bit more welcome in white settings. Women of all backgrounds are more distinctly set apart from men than they were twenty years ago.

Occupational Prestige

Another useful indicator of economic equality is occupational prestige, or the honor, social esteem, and standing assigned to workers in an occupation by the society at large. Sociologists have devised highly reliable scales of jobs from 0 to 100, low to high, based upon public attitudes.[9] Thus a maid scores 11, an auto mechanic 37, a nurse 54, and a lawyer 76. (The lowest-ranking common occupation is farm laborer with 10, the highest, physician, with 88.) By this measure, white women have prestige scores close to men, because the bulk of clerical jobs fall in the middle of the prestige range. Minority women, on the other hand, have lost ground in the seventies. Black, Native American, Mexican-American, and Puerto Rican males all have lower scores than whites on the average, although they have gained small ground in recent years.

Putting prestige distributions together with occupational segregation, two conclusions appear. First, women and minorities are getting different jobs than white men. Second, the jobs they get are valued less overall by society.

Income

No item is more important ultimately to individual workers than paycheck size. The garbage collector can forego social esteem for a comfortable salary. The seamstress does not mind that her coworkers are all women so long as the piece rate is fair. Construction workers trade year-round employment for a high hourly wage scale. It is conceivable to think that a society is just where groups monopolize particular jobs yet all reap similar rewards. "Fair pay," "equal pay for equal work," and "equal reward for equal preparation" are what matter, not the context of the job.

When we examine income trends over the past thirty years, the conclusions are clear-cut. First, the wages of nonwhites since the days of civil rights activism have been increasing at a faster rate than those of whites. In 1960, the average black man earned $5700 a year, compared to $10,400 for white men; by 1974 his salary leapt to $9100 compared to the white's $12,400. These are significant and incontrovertible gains, which, however, must be seen in light of more sobering facts. One is that black men were so poorly paid to begin with that any improvement seems massive; in relative terms, they still earn about 75 cents for every dollar earned by a white. (This is a small gain since the days of the American revolution, when a black man was evaluated at three-fifths, or, in economic terms, 60 cents for every dollar of a white.) In addition, if we were to presume these rates of increase continue, which is questionable, it would still take several generations for minority men to reach parity with whites.

While nonwhite males are benefiting at the pay booths, women of all races are falling behind. Men earn considerably more than women, and the gap between incomes is steadily increasing. In 1979, women workers earned about 56 cents for every dollar a man brought home. In other words, our society values women's labor at about half that of white men. Currently all women, regardless of color or ethnicity, earn similarly low wages. A white woman with a college degree takes home less money than a minority male high school dropout.

These sex differences persist no matter how fine the distinctions one draws. One can separate out only full-time workers or highly educated workers or workers with the same amount of experience in a job—the men will receive the profits of their gender. Furthermore, men get more frequent and larger raises over their lifetime. Thus a full-time woman worker can look back over forty years of labor and discover that she has earned *a quarter of a million dollars* less than a comparable male in her field. Economic inequality is not disappearing at a rapid rate. In spite of civil rights programs and policies, "affirmative-action" hiring, federal and state regulations, and less public prejudice, both minority races and women lack significant opportunities and rewards. Racial minorities are particularly hampered at job entry, having twice the unemployment rate of whites.

Women are disadvantaged when they open their slender pay envelopes.

Simply put, the rules remain "Don't let so many blacks in" or "Hire them only for temporary work," and "If you hire a woman, don't pay her well."

Some improvements can be admitted to—better jobs opening up for a few nonwhites and females, the earnings of minorities overall increasing. But there is no indication that white males are losing jobs or wages as a result of these few gains. Indeed, the job situation for white males continues, as it has for decades, to acquire an increasingly privileged position: low unemployment during slow periods, and movement from unskilled jobs to managerial or professional ones.

In light of these data, to argue "reverse discrimination" is ludicrous. Women and minorities have so far to go just to catch up with most white men today—if one wants to use that as a base for equality—that rather massive economic changes will be required to have a system of equality.

STATISTICAL SUBVERSION

Why do so many believe the United States has achieved equality? A prime source of the myth rests with the government and university researchers, who misrepresent or distort the facts, and the media, who report them uncritically.

All statistics have weaknesses. What is striking about the ones discussed here is that they all *underestimate* the economic disparity between white males and others.

Consider the unemployment measure. Throughout each year, the federal government runs a Current Population Survey, a type of continual census, based upon a sample of the nation's population. During the interview, people are asked whether anyone in their household made a specific effort to find a job the previous week. The interviewer does not mention the word "unemployed" at all. The Labor Department then categorizes these cases by age, sex, and race, and uses the totals to calculate the various unemployment rates.[10]

The procedure undercounts the actual number of unemployed in several ways. First, the interviewers throw out of the count any job hunters with mental or physical disabilities. Approximately five to seven million people in this country have such impairments, so to ignore them is no small exclusion. Second, the questions do not catch other types of unemployed people. For example, they ignore the discouraged long-term unemployed worker who has in despair or resignation given up an active job hunt. They leave out, too, the seasonal workers who would rather work year-round, or the part-time workers who would rather work full-time. Finally, they overlook the housewives who may dream of a job, yet are too isolated from the work world to know how to enter or develop the skills for entering.

That more people are willing and able to take on jobs than the unemployment statistics indicate, was proved in a study by Rutgers University researchers, who wanted to compare the official unemployment rate with the actual one.[11] To do this, they selected New Brunswick, New Jersey, a city with both

black and white (largely Hungarian) poverty areas. In order to
carry out their interviews, they went to the kinds of extremes
that federal investigators are likely to adopt: yelling through
doors to the urban-frightened, deferring to a doorman at expensive highrises to let them enter a building, chatting with al-
coholics on streets, finding a Magyar-speaking assistant to
question the Hungarians. They asked people whether they had
a job, if it was part-time or full-time, and whether they wanted
to be working full-time.

To count the unemployed, they first eliminated the retired,
married housewives, and strikers seeking work. They ended up
counting all adults with a job history who were out of work, yet
willing to work. According to official figures at the time, the unemployment rate for the area was about 9 percent. But the
Rutgers researchers found that it was closer to 16 percent. Most
disturbing, they discovered that almost 60 percent of the population was without a full-time job. About half of these were
part-time workers who wanted more work.

To conclude, unemployment statistics tell us only about the
most employable portion of the adult population. They mask
the real work fates of the disabled, the foreign-language speakers, and many of the poor with wages from part-time work. Yet
in spite of these errors, it is clear that "reverse discrimination"
is not keeping minorities off the unemployment lines.

For occupational assignment, census categories have become
standard in research. According to all studies, both minorities
and women are now close to white males in the proportion of
the highest classification, "Professional-Technical." But this includes lab technicians and lawyers, kindergarten teachers and
architects. It even includes artists, dancers, and writers. The
women and blacks in this category are not doctors, engineers,
or chemists, as the classification seems to imply; rather they are
social workers, teachers, or nurses, who earn much less and
enjoy little job autonomy. Consequently, it is wrong to conclude they have reached parity with white men.

The prestige scale is the most popular measure of success
among sociologists, who like to report that women and men
enjoy almost identical job standing. The problem is that the
surveys that form the basis of the scale refer to the imaginary

worker being rated as a male. It is open to test whether or not women doctors enjoy the same esteem and respect as male, but researchers have chosen to sidestep this check and assume otherwise.

That sociologists concentrate upon studying occupational prestige, probably the least salient job quality to workers, rather than income, unemployment, or job assignment, itself suggests an unwillingness on their part to face the facts of disadvantage, discrimination, and poverty in this country. They are like the early explorers who, upon approaching their first iceberg, concluded upon observation of its tip that it wasn't so bad.

Finally, in considering income disparities, it must be remembered that the better-paying jobs include benefit packages of considerable financial value. Management jobs especially can include such "perks" as rental cars, entertainment expense money, stock options, and so on. Were these calculated at value and added to earnings, there is no doubt that the total job rewards accrued to white males compared to the other groups would be larger.

Distortion of data by government and science has been accompanied by self-selection or censorship by the media. Most people today know the names of Brian Weber or Allan Bakke, but who knows the identity of the stewardess who successfully won the overturning of the age requirement for flight attendant work, or the black man who had unfair test procedures tossed out of the personnel offices? The press has not made celebrities out of any of these people.

Nor have the news media reported accurately on the effects of affirmative action policies. *Fortune* magazine was quick to publish the expenses of the consent decree that required AT&T to pay $18 million in retributions to employees who had been underpaid or kept from promotion in the past.[12] It also quoted extensively from white men who were embittered by the situation and believed themselves at a disadvantage. However, it failed to report that as a result of AT&T's job reorganization, men came out as the beneficiaries.[13] Men as a group gained 14,-000 jobs while women lost 22,000. Over 16,000 men moved into formerly women's work, while only 9,400 women moved into formerly men's jobs. And although Bell has gotten much media play out of its advertisements portraying women pole climbers and installers, it has failed to disclose that these jobs will soon be eliminated by new technology. In other words, Bell has used affirmative action to its advantage—to put women in men's jobs that were going to be shut out anyway, and transfer men into higher, more secure positions.

MISSING VICTIMS

The information presented so far has described the plight of minorities, particularly blacks and women, as victims of the system of inequality. The Bakke case is important because it brought to public view the fact that other people also face disadvantage and handicaps. Certainly not all white men are equal in our society. A coal miner's son from Appalachia has little better chance of making it to an Ivy League college than the child of a black laundry worker. Sons of various Hispanic groups—Chicano, Puerto Rican, Cuban—may appear white and speak standard English, but this does not guarantee they, as a Rodriguez or Garcia, will be accepted by personnel interviewers the same way as a Roberts or a Sorensen. Enough Polish, Italian, and Jewish people have faced the closing doors of discrimination that each of these groups now has antidefamation organizations.

During the Bakke case, some of these groups argued that society did not seem to notice that they too had difficulties finding spaces in medical schools. One reason for this lack of concern, they argued, was simply the absence of information. The National Polish Congress noted correctly that aside from Hispanics, "very little data, if any, has been collected indicating what problems, if any, we [white ethnics] face with respect to religious and national origin discrimination."[14] Indeed, the government and social science data banks relating to economic discrimination deal almost exclusively with women and blacks, so my reference primarily to these groups does not reflect a bias on my part. The data on others is virtually unavailable.

Consequently, the public has been must misled about the facts of poverty. When asked to conjure up a typical welfare case, most people would probably visualize a black mother and her children. In fact, *the most typical poor household in our country is white and an adult male resides within it.* Consider these figures from the 1970 Census count of people living below the poverty level:

Whites in two-adult families	10.3 million
Whites in female-headed families	1.8 million
Blacks in two-adult families	3.6 million
Blacks in female-headed families	3.1 million

Obviously starchy diets and crowded apartments are not facts of life reserved for blacks.

Yet, others face difficulties in the labor market as well, notably the handicapped and the aged. Again, our knowledge of these persons' subordinacy comes from their public announcements and political activism of recent years, not from the statistical archives. In fact, we have seen how the government deflates the real unemployment figures by ignoring the disabled. And though employment discrimination on the basis of age is forbidden by various federal regulations, many people over forty can describe an instance in which they have been unfairly treated by employers.

To acknowledge that characteristics other than a female body or dark skin provoke subjugation may leave us in a quandary in our search for understanding inequality. Since so little exists in the way of substantial figures on other groups, we cannot study them in detail.[15] Yet to rely upon the well-documented cases of women and blacks is to perpetuate the idea that only these two groups provide victims.

The solution is to take what facts we do have and consider how they point to general patterns of excluding people regardless of the basis for the exclusion. Thus, the rationalizations and practices a hirer invokes to overlook a woman for a position probably share many qualities with those he or she uses to pass up a veteran in a wheelchair or a middle-aged man who speaks with an accent. Similarly, the assumptions policy makers form about the work force when they design plans to advance blacks will apply to other workers as well.

Finally, to concentrate on women and blacks is to consider the most prevalent forms of discrimination, which affect more than half the work force today. Still, we must remember that this group is joined by others, like Allan Bakke, who though fewer and less visible, are also kept under by unfair plays in the game of achievement.

Chapter 4

Unnatural Deceptions

It is a plain, simple fact that women have shown themselves naturally incompetent to fill a great many of the business positions which they have sought to occupy.

Edward Bok, Ladies Home Journal, *1900*

Professor Henry Goddard's 1912 study, sponsored by the U.S. Immigration Service, found that 83 percent of Jews, 80 percent of Hungarians, 79 percent of Italians, and 87 percent of Russians were feeble-minded, based on "culture free" tests.

Samuel Bowles and Herbert Gintis,
Schooling in Capitalist America

The Negro has the lower mental faculties (smell, sight, handicraftsmanship, body sense, melody) well-developed, the Caucasian the higher (self-control, will power, ethical and aesthetic senses and reason).

Robert Bennett Dean, American Journal
of Anatomy, *1906*

If the American Dream does not work for the majority of workers, then it is important that the culture have built within it a rationale for the failures. Our Puritan base provides two major explanations for the inequality in a society built upon equals. In this chapter we shall explore how conceptions about the natural order of life demand systems of hierarchy; in the next, how individual sin brings about lesser rewards.

Western culture has a preoccupation with ranking. The divisions of heaven and hell, saints and sinners, God and humans, humans and beasts pervaded medieval thought, just as rich and poor, celebrity and nobody, leader and follower, or coach and players suffuse contemporary imagery. The question then is how the rich, celebrities, leaders, and coaches turned out to be white males. The simplest answer from the culture is that they are more fit and competent.

The best strategy for establishing ruling class superiority is an offensive one—to provide that others are by plan of nature not suited for high positions. This models the paternalism of Puritan government, for if a man be born with no more ability than that of a sheep herder, he could work happy knowing he was in his calling, and sleep well aware that the governor was a man of great qualification. This attitude takes the blame off people for failure by a sleight-of-hand suggestion that failure doesn't exist. It also can be used to remind (or force) people to stay in their place.

With the waning of Puritanism, the privileged class in society required a new set of interpretations to replace religious ones. The result was the growth of secular prejudices toward groups of people, a set of attitudes backed up by some respectable authority. The most obvious case is racism toward blacks. Derogatory attitudes did not spring up overnight; they sprouted slowly as the ruling political and economic interests themselves became aware of the profit in subjugating the black population.

ANXIOUS OPPRESSION

The roots of prejudice toward nonwhites in the United States can be found in the first English confrontations with Africans.[1] The first English voyagers to Africa arrived around 1550 to trade with the natives; slavery was not in the English adventurers' minds for some decades afterwards. While they approached the Africans as merely another sort of people, they could not help but come to see them as peculiar, and ultimately repulsive.

Although Africans come in many shades of color, the English saw only one shade. "These people are all blacke, and are called Negros, without any apparell, saving before their privities."[2] At that time no color conveyed so much emotional impact, all negative in connotation: death, disaster, wickedness, disgrace, evil, ugliness, sin, filth, the devil. Where at first the English found the difference in appearance a curiosity, even a marvel, eventually the symbolism of their language established the base for a philosophy relegating other races to inferior status.

It was the tragic fate of Africans as well to be living in a country that was the habitat of large tailless apes who walked about like humans. Consequently, when the English found themselves face to face with orangutans on the one hand and Africans on the other, they drew conclusions of similarity. A few observers deduced that the Africans had sprung up from apes, or that apes were the offspring of Africans and another unknown beast. The most common speculation was that "a beastly copulation or conjecture" occurred between the two.

Given this beastly connection, it was a short step for the Elizabethans to venal sexuality. Thus they avidly sopped up any evidence of African "lechery," be it multiple wives, sanctioned homosexuality, nudity, or sex out of marriage. Travelers wrote home of African men's "large propagators" as physical proof of their lust.

Other signs of African savagery, or failure to behave in a "civilized" manner, appeared in chronicles. Various tribes were reported to practice ritual murder, infanticide, and cosmetic mutilation—acts the Elizabethans pretended did not exist in their own culture. Just as shocking, Africans were said to live in mud or straw huts, eat with their hands, and dine on unusual foods. That the Africans structured their government around kings and nobles was taken as one sign they were not totally inhuman—though this quality was soon overlooked.

Representing yet another defect or impropriety, the "heathen" religions of the Africans threatened English Christians. Paradoxically, while religious leaders searched for similarities between African and Christian spiritual practices, they militated against the unity of humankind and the conversion of their darker kin.

Overall, English attitudes encouraged segregation of themselves from Africans, though not domination over them. In 1619 "twenty Negars" sold to the Jamestown colony marked the introduction of blacks into America. Very likely they were treated no differently at first than white indentured servants. But soon property owners saw the dark skin to have a special value, as it immediately marked a man as of a particular status, in this case as slaves. By 1660, economic interests saw that slavery was legitimate in law.

Prejudice against Africans and the emerging institution of slavery intertwined and reinforced each other, sending blacks down the road to total subjugation and degradation. By the time of independence, Southern agricultural and Northern trading interests were convinced of the necessity of slavery. For the average white American, the stereotype of the lazy, lustful, dim-witted black loomed in their minds, allowing them to fight for equality so long as it did not mean the equality of lesser humans. Where in Puritan times God's order was a hierarchy of white men bound reciprocally to one another, the new order was equality among free white men in dominance of blacks.

Following independence, Americans were in a dilemma. On the one hand, they held as their creed that all were equal under God, hence due rights inherent and inalienable. On the other, they believed slavery an economic necessity and that women should not participate in government. This conflict was epitomized at the time in the writing and behavior of Thomas Jefferson, who so eloquently stated the nation's commitment to freedom from tyranny, abhorred the injustice of slavery, yet maintained his own plantation. In his widely read *Notes on Virginia*, Jefferson's solution was a convenient confusion: he allowed that blacks had the moral sense of human beings (though it be suppressed by slavery) while being inherently different from whites in temperament and inclination.[3]

Of most serious import for black future were Jefferson's remarks on mental capacity. "In reason much inferior, as I think one could scarcely be found capable of tracing and comprehending the investigations of Euclid; and that in imagination they are dull, tasteless, and anomalous." Toward the end of his commentary, perhaps aware that he was overstating facts, Jefferson passed the issue over to American science. "To justify a general conclusion requires many observations." This delivery of a moral decision to the hands of science was a quintessentially American step, and, as we now know, a foolhardy one.

In response to Jefferson's call, scientists took up the classification of human types on a racial basis. Body snatchers skulked at night to find corpses for the measurement of skulls, legs, and breasts. Dr. Charles White's influential book in 1799 catalogued the many ways in which blacks seemed closer to apes than to whites. There he disclosed "That the PENIS of an African is larger than that of an European has, I believe, been shown in every anatomical school in London."[4] Antislavery writers valiantly, though unsuccessfully, tried to convince the public of the errors in such studies. They were, however, able to convince enough people to fight to abolish slavery.

A GARDEN OF PREJUDICE

With the institution of slavery destroyed, from its ashes rose a pernicious, invidious system of racism, which bound blacks to inferior status and rights throughout society—in churches, at work, in communities. By the end of the nineteenth century, the "proof by natural differences" revived with the support of the theory of evolution.

It had been demonstrated by the preeminent social philosopher of the times, Herbert Spencer, that some races of humanity were better equipped than others.[5] According to his theory, which was widely read and discussed by the populace, one could identify a hierarchy of development within the human species similar to the phylogenetic ladder that classified all creatures. If the human perched at the top of the animal pyramid, the white Aryan and Anglo-Saxon sat on the pinnacle of human development. Other whites, Slavs or Latins in particular, were "inferior races," yet more advanced than the "savages," Indians, Mexicans, Africans, and Asians. The Jews were thought to be a distinct race themselves, one characterized as "moral cripples, their souls warped and dwarfed," according to sociologist E. A. Ross.[6]

As representatives of a lower stage of biological evolution, the "savage" and "semicivilized" peoples lacked the mental, physical, or moral traits required for the leadership of society. They were not to be blamed for their inferiority, as it was an accident of birth. Indeed, it became the popular belief that good Christian "superiors" should do what they could to "civilize" these wretches. This ideology was most nurturing of the imperialist expansions into native cultures at the time—the overthrow of Queen Lillioukeana in Hawaii, the destruction of cultures throughout the South Seas, the incursions into sugar-growing islands in the Caribbean.

Within the nation social Darwinism bolstered race hatred of whites toward blacks and competition among the old and new immigrant groups. These attitudes are immediately apparent upon looking at the most respectable newspapers of the period.

Jews could be labelled "sheenies," Irish "micks." Cartoons regularly featured foot-shuffling, eye-rolling, ignorant blacks with massive, drooping lips. Southern and Eastern Europeans were depicted as superstitious and impassioned, too blindly enthusiastic to be trusted. The heroes of these pages were the self-reliant, self-disciplined white Anglo-Saxon Protestants.

If in fact the races fit such descriptions, then the social order of the society, bursting at its seams from the growing population, economy, industrialization, and urbanization, was a simple one. One need only assort people by their level of ability. Indeed, according to the censuses of these years, this is what was happening. Managers, proprietors, and farmers were of the favored white stock. In government and small businesses one heard the accents of later arrivals such as the Irish. Further down, amid the noise and dirt of the factory or the dust and dank of the sweatshop, languages of recent immigrants rang out. At places of hard labor or in homes as servants, the blacks sought their meager wages. The Indians were dead.

Belief in racial superiority permeated all parts of the political spectrum. Socialists and reformers accepted this law of nature along with conservative businessmen who profited so much from its workings. The socialist novelist Jack London littered his books with brawny blond men and women who outwitted natives in their own world and led the working class, in his eyes incapable of ruling itself, out of oppression. Theodore Roosevelt, hardly a conservative President, once announced, "I don't go so far as to say that the only good Indians are dead Indians, but nine out of ten are, and I shouldn't inquire too closely into the case of the tenth."[7]

Those born since 1950 probably cannot fathom the pervasiveness of racism and ethnic prejudice throughout the society—the blatant stereotypes of the newspapers and magazines, the derogatory epithets, the flippant sayings tossed in daily conversations, the frequent inclusion of words such as "nigger" in respectable persons' vocabularies. Such surface appearances of racism have now vanished to the extent that persons of prominence who use racial slurs are roundly criticized or even asked to leave office.

It should come as no surprise too that the belief in female inferiority also has strong roots in American society. Indeed, what is novel about the latest resurgence of feminism is that its advocates hold women to be equal to men.[8] By contrast, most suffragettes held the prevalent belief that women were different from men, not as well-endowed in intellectual faculties, and limited by their "organic" peculiarities, their wombs with their hysterical emanations. Women deserved the vote, they argued, because they were superior in one regard to men—in moral purity—hence would bring more peace to a discordant society.

Women were thought to share many of the weaknesses of the inferior racial groups—the passions of the Latins, the mysteriousness of the Slavs, the ignorance and weak self-discipline of the Negroes. As with the races, they could be assorted into their proper place. For white middle-class women, this meant at home with children, in the service of the husband's rule. For other women, it meant arduous labor paid at rates much less than working-class men. As spiritual beings, women were held to be above material concerns, dependent upon the men, who could, in fact, better provide for their welfare.

These racist and sexist strands wove a strong pattern in American culture, offering an obvious explanation as to why only certain types of Americans won fame and riches. Distinguished scientists, noted doctors, respected ministers, and esteemed academics were quick to offer proof of the inferiority of all but the white Anglo-Saxon male. Only he, they claimed, had the vigor, fortitude, wit, and courage to rule a nation teeming with cities and factories. The others, deficient beings, deserved little for their labor, and could expect relief from daily struggle only through the benevolent exercise of the elite.

THE NEW SOCIAL DARWINISM

The legacy of prejudice has not been severed by recent civil-rights activities. Too many people believe it is to their advantage to denigrate and exclude other groups from education, jobs, and neighborhoods. Intellectuals fear that the newcomers will ruin the quality of education. Employers presume it is to their economic advantage to maintain a large overqualified, underpaid work force. Homeowners worry that the introduction of neighbors of different background or appearance will weaken their property investments and disturb their way of life. In the area of sex relations, men resist sharing their lives with women who display competence, skill, and personal strength, and instead insist that dominance is a survival need of the male creature.

Television, movies, radio, and their supporting advertisements reinforce these expressions of insecurity. The outlandish portrayals of mammies, bucks, and coons remain, disguised only slightly by updated clothing and speech patterns. The fictitious women of the media are still dumb blonds, housewives neurotically obsessed with cleanliness, and nubile vapid models. Italians are working-class toughs, on the verge of either explosive violence or a song. Hispanics talk funny and think the world is one big laugh. People with disabilities, middle-aged women, and Native Americans don't exist. Were an anthropologist of the year 3000 to describe our population on the basis of some media samplings, she would describe it with a mechanically rigid set of categories, not the rich panoply of personalities, cultures, and styles that comprise our polyglot society.

By portraying certain groups in very narrow ways, the media foster the attitude that members of the group are unfit for other activities. The most serious damage is to the children, who lack the wisdom to discern the inaccuracies of the television and movie world, and who narrow their vision of opportunities for themselves and others in response.

The issue of stereotyping is complex. In a society such as ours, with large populations of many historical backgrounds, stereotyping serves social order. To cast others as different is to affirm one's own values and way of looking at the world. Stereotyping encourages a we-feeling and cohesiveness among the name callers. So it is not surprising that even today, Americans are quick to claim that Germans are militarists, Chinese clannish, Jews education-oriented, Irish patriotic, Italians festive, blacks easygoing, and women emotional.[9] Members of these various groups may very well agree, although they might interpret the description as a source of pride, not one of insult.

The problem is less with the stereotyping than the fact that some groups have more power and resources in society, hence their impressions of others will affect the direction of important decisions. So it is the stereotypes held by employers, usually white men of privilege, that weigh in the allocation of jobs, salaries, and benefits to people. It is this group's self-perceptions that set the tone for the definition of a good worker—and that is one who is cool, aggressive, competitive, and materialistic—a model WASP male. The validity of this belief is beside the point to employers, who ignore the possibility that these traits may make for poor performance on some jobs. The mythical John Wayne manager is still the ideal for administrative positions, even though we now know that this leadership style has flaws.

Stereotypes also serve as blinders in the evaluation of workers. The personnel manager who believes Italians are quick-tempered and overly committed to family life is more likely to pick up these characteristics in an Italian worker, even though they may in fact be no more extreme than would be displayed by someone from a different ethnic background. Since the traits seem to fit, they are the ones that become salient in the observer's eyes. Similarly, a stereotype can direct a manager to see a trait when it doesn't exist, for example, to believe that a black worker is stronger or more physically adept than other workers on a team when this is not the case. Most important, by directing the manager to a limited set of qualities, stereotypes misdirect him from a fair evaluation of those behaviors and inclinations that are most appropriate for the job at hand.

As in the past, the decision makers of today can rely upon the conclusions of academics and scientists for support in typing people. Where medical doctors once measured penises and weighed brains, psychologists now tally IQs and scores on personality inventories. Though based on a dubious theory of ability, the measurement of cranial cavities at least had the advantage of being reliable and valid. Several scientists with calipers could quibble over a centimeter or two at the most in examination of the same skull. The reliability and meaning of today's psychological tests are more conjectural. In extreme form, as represented by the writings of William Shockley or Arthur Jensen, the scientist purporting racial differences in IQ barely disguises his desire to subjugate nonwhites.[10] These articles perfectly match the mentality of the turn-of-the-century social Darwinists.

The simplest rebuttal of physical difference by race is the reminder that race as a concept is more complex than these investigators presume. Jensen correctly argues that races are "breeding populations," which means they consist of bodies of people who have interbred over many generations within a relatively circumscribed area. Consequently, anthropologists who use the term "race" refer to over thirty groups of people around the world that form distinct breeding pools. This means that skin color is not a good basis for defining race, for in the United States each white person among a handful at a party could come from a different race. Jensen ignored this variation in his studies, and simply divided his research samples into black and white subjects. His next error was to subsume all blacks together. Not only do people of color derive from different breeding populations, many in the United States have Caucasian influences in their genes as a result of interracial marriages, love affairs, and rapes.

Because skin color is a poor basis for distinguishing groups of people physiologically, sophisticated researchers attribute differences between whites and blacks in the United States to their varying history, culture, economic conditions, and political power. Even this approach has encouraged the reinforcement of stereotyping. For example, in the sixties a popular explanation for black unemployment was the "culture of poverty," which purportedly left people unmotivated, hedonistic, and exploitative—hardly qualities employers want from workers. The implication was that blacks behaved weirdly, that their strange values and actions were as unmistakable as fingerprints. Although critics later pointed out that anyone living in rat-infested, filth-ridden tenements far from factories and offices is prone to live life for today, the belief remains that the country has large bodies of intractable and potentially violent blacks. When people of similar appearance (similar in whites' eyes, that is) remain poor for several generations, the conclusion drawn by the average person is that poverty is in the people's blood.

To argue that differences between the sexes are not natural and therefore immutable seems more difficult. Indisputable differences in mature body appearance and physiological functioning are obvious. One could point out that female and male, as God made them, are remarkably similar, bearing two eyes, legs, arms, and an assortment of identical internal organs. One could note that all humans as fetuses begin life with a proclivity for being female, that adult males carry the remnants of a uterus within their penis and can, under the right conditions, give milk from their breasts. One could show that the normal flushes and falls of the hormones during a lifetime can change a hard, virile youth into a soft-breasted man of maturity.[11] Biologists can point to other kinds of evidence that "male" and "female" are the ends of a continuum, not absolute categories. When presented to a society that insists upon shoving people and objects into segregated categories, these facts are almost incomprehensible. Consequently, researchers who would accept that whites and blacks are not physiologically different rest naively secure that at least men and women are totally separate creatures.

The driving force behind most of these claims has been testosterone, the male hormone, which is said to be the source of male aggression, hence their natural basis for leadership. Sociologist Steven Goldberg argues this is why "there are more brilliant men than brilliant women and more powerful men than powerful women."[12] Now the data upon which such statements are made is highly suspect. But even if we accept the results as completely valid, they would seem to suggest something very different from the researchers' claims. The data on male aggression show that men attack other men, while women attack neither other women nor men. Brute force is hardly a good characteristic for the managers of schools, hospitals, factories, offices, and governments. The people who insist on the validity of these studies are playing word games to hoodwink the lay public into believing that men are naturally superior.

Let us take a more conservative tack, and presume that some of the research demonstrating female-male differences in personality, skills, and interests are valid. Given nature's tendency to differentiate objects, it is reasonable that some genuine distinctions are present. When one looks over the dissemination of this information and the way it is presented to or interpreted by the public, a set of errors emerge, all of which are made in behalf of making men look more competent than women.

A curious practice in science is to ignore findings where no differences emerge between studied groups. In fact, a researcher who comes up with these so-called "negative findings" is likely to have difficulty publishing her results. Typically, a psychologist will test women and men on a variety of skills or aptitudes and find differences in one or two. Then she will make great play of this information and ignore that in over ninety percent of her tests, no differences occurred.[13] For example, in research on children's play behavior, much has been written about the fact that boys are more active on playgrounds than girls. But hardly anything has been said about all the data showing that for the most part boys and girls play alike in many ways and with the same toys.[14] In terms of the overall picture the differences are trivial, a small and interesting variation. Although the fact that women and men have few differences in traits and skills is a fascinating and important finding, researchers continue to ignore this fact and thus mislead the general public as to the real state of the sexes in our society.

Consider now that small set of differences that do seem to appear in one study after another, regardless of the exact dimensions of the experiment or the backgrounds of women and men in the sample. For example, it is often reported that males score better on mathematical aptitude tests. Many interpret such data to mean that men are better than women at numbers, and are naturally better engineers, scientists, and architects. Assuming the tests are valid, this conclusion is utterly erroneous. First, the difference in test scores may be persistent—that is, large groups of men score higher on the average than large groups of women—yet of practical insignificance. The men's scores may only differ in one or two items in order for the scientists to label the difference as real. Second, the scores of individual men and women will have great overlap, such that many individual women will score better than individual men; there will be women of striking mathematical talent and men who get confused over long division.

The consequences of this erroneous reasoning are all around us. Since only boys are encouraged in professions such as engineering, a number of those admitted will not have the level of basic competence and motivation of some girls. While Jim Frank designs a bridge that collapses and his brother Al discovers that his new automobile design bears a serious structural flaw, their mathematically gifted sister Susan types invoice forms and serves coffee. A highly technological society cannot afford such a sloppy basis for assigning people to jobs. To do so guarantees inefficiency and failure, that all the best minds are not being applied to the problems we face in supplying food, reducing pollution, and developing efficient energy uses.

If the translations of scientific results to the public are faulty, so too the facts selected for report are of a particular kind. Only those sex differences that favor the position of men hit the pages of newspapers and magazines. For example, the human engineers at the Johnson O'Connor Research Foundation have in their half century of experience identified six work aptitudes at which women consistently score higher overall as a group than men.[15] Men excel in only two—Grip, a measure of physical energy, and Structural Visualization, the ability to construct three-dimensional puzzles. (On thirteen aptitudes no sex differences appear.) It is doubtful whether any reader of this book could name more than one of the female aptitudes; this ignorance reflects selective reporting. Similarly, the media are quick to report what are defined to be female deficiencies. For example, while writing this book I saw several news items reporting that women had smaller thumbs than men, and thus were not qualified for certain well-paid crafts jobs in Germany. Later someone from the Silicone Valley in California, a region where microcircuits are constructed, told me the companies there use the fact of women's so-called short thumbs to place them in low-paid assembly work. Here a "defect" is used as an excuse to keep women in dead-end labor. Obviously the employers would be obtaining a better labor force simply by measuring applicants' thumbs; they avoid doing this because were they to hire men for the work, the salaries would necessarily rise. Finally, unusual instances like thumb length aside, most skills, interests, and aptitudes that differentiate the sexes are malleable. Women can increase their grip through exercise; men can extend their finger dexterity with practice, as surgeons do by needlepointing between operations. If boys and girls in our society had identical experiences and opportunities, then the few differences now found between women and men would probably be reduced to an infinitesimal number.

A brief excursion into science fiction illustrates the absurdity of our approach to typecasting people on the basis of erroneous interpretations. Imagine that you are at a library in the year 2050, and you punch a button for the computer to give you information on work in the United States. The following passage prints up on the cathode tube:

> *In 1985 the President's Special Commission on Natural Differences reported its findings, which resulted in a tumultous redesign of work within the country. This blue ribbon panel of scientists proved definitely that women's superiority in many areas should be put to use in the labor force. Among their implemented suggestions were the following:*
>
> * *Because women live longer than men, they should be given preference in positions requiring lengthy training, such as medicine, science, and law. For this reason too, they should not be paid less than men on the presumption that their career life is shorter; longevity compensates for a few years of childbearing.*
> * *Since women are more facile with words, they should take over publishing houses, news media, and the literary arts.*
> * *Given women's superiority at learning languages and technical systems, they should have the major opportunities in sciences like chemistry, biology, botany, and anatomy.*
> * *Women's exceptional abstract visualization earns them preferred places in banking, management, and politics.*
> * *Given their finger dexterity and short thumbs, women should make the best surgeons.*
> * *In view of their outstanding accounting aptitude, women should run all actuarial, statistical, and financial departments of organizations.*
> * *Because women are exceptionally strong in persuasive skills, they should be given all highly competitive sales jobs, such as*

> *those in the fields of automobiles, computers, machinery, and basic resources. Since men are less skillful here, they can sell food, clothes, and everyday necessities.*
> - *Given men's physical strength and proficiency, they should handle the majority of household tasks, which require constant bending, stretching, lifting of weights (groceries, laundry, and children), and lung capacity.*
> - *Because men are better at constructing objects, they can work best as the assistants to women in laboratories, implementing the physical tasks in support of women's theoretical creations.*
> - *Men's tendency to fight one another requires that they be under the supervision of women managers, who are more skillful at preventing and resolving conflicts. Men will staff the infantry under female leadership.*

All the conclusions in this imaginary passage are reasonable in light of our knowledge of women and men to date—provided one follows the erroneous ways of those who claim men are superior. The same illogic applies as well to discussions of differences between blacks and whites, Japanese and Native Americans, Greeks and Norwegians.

Stereotypes affect scientists no less than the rest of us. Even when researchers are sensitive to this possibility, others will twist their findings to fit preferable themes in our culture. Regardless of the origins of the distortions, the effect is the same: to discredit one group or another for the benefit of the success mythology. Many writers of the Constitution must be smiling from their graves in agreement: all white men are created equal and endowed by their Creator with inalienable rights. Science tells us so.

Chapter 5

Blaming
the Victim

[Of blacks] the evidence is now all too clear that the qualified (and a good number of the unqualified, too) get jobs and admissions. It is one thing to be asked to fight discrimination against the competent, hard-working, and law-abiding; it is quite another to be asked to fight discrimination against the less competent or incompetent and criminally inclined.

Nathan Glazer, Affirmative Discrimination

When I ask businessmen to find jobs for young blacks, they say, "No, we cannot afford to as long as there is a pool of better qualified whites to draw from."

Carl Hollman, President,
National Urban Coalition

In this age of narcissism, Americans believe the poor are to blame for their own troubles. In one national survey, the leading reasons given for poverty were lack of thrift, lack of effort, lack of ability, and loose morals. Much less frequently mentioned were inadequate schools, low wages, or the failure of private industry to provide jobs.[1] The better off people are, the more they attribute poverty to lack of hard work and low motivation, whereas poor people themselves think they've worked as hard as everyone else and point instead to the social and economic systems as culprits.[2] And well-educated people, who often find their political views liberalized during college, where they gain more understanding of social and historical forces upon individuals, grow more conservative as their diplomas place them in well-paying, powerful jobs.[3] Consequently, those people who make decisions about social welfare in our society are the most individualistic and most disinclined to consider social dynamics.

Since economists and social scientists are among the elect, the best of the white males in their own (and others') eyes, then it follows that many scientific explanations for discrimination are variations on the popular theme that women and minorities are only getting their fair due, which, given their inferiority, is justly less. For example, a mass of social science writing argues that ghetto life produces people, in Edward Banfield's words, "unable or unwilling to control impulses or put forth any effort at self-improvement."[4] Nathan Glazer and Daniel P. Moynihan ask, "What are we to do with the large number of people emerging in modern society who are irresponsible and depraved? The worthy poor create no serious problems—nothing that money cannot solve. But the unworthy poor? No one has come up with the answers."[5] These writers turn Jefferson on his head in suggesting that some blacks are beyond salvation, hence their disadvantaged position is fair and equitable.

Though presumably learned and eminent scholars, Banfield, Glazer, Moynihan, and other neoconservatives who have expressed similar sentiments never identify what "unworthiness" consists of, and in implying that it is a characteristic of the ghetto, attribute it to blacks as a group. Assuredly these men would agree that whites can be "unworthy" too, though they neglect to mention this possibility. Thus they feed the more blatant racism of those who seek proof that blacks are inferior.

Such silvery statements remind us how not all that slips forth from scientists' mouths is scientific. Just what makes someone "irresponsible and depraved?" How do we identify people "unwilling to help themselves?" Glib and vague terms, they elude measurement. None can disprove the ideas, for none can test them. Thus they stand, without any support in fact, while persons of intelligence accept them on faith as mirrors of reality.

A more convincing form of blaming-the-victim-theory pervades economics and policy making today. According to this view, often called the "human capital theory" of inequality, workers are merely another form of capital. Hence, an employer can weigh the value of one worker against another just as he can evaluate different material supplies.[6] For example, a talented athlete of little musical ability is not worth a cent in the symphony orchestra market, but may have a six-figure income potential on the golfing circuit. People have many capabilities, and by investing in themselves, they can develop certain talents to become high producers in particular occupations.

Workers can increase their capital in several ways. The most frequent tactic is to acquire additional education or vocational training. They can simply stay with a job and accumulate experience. They can also study the labor market and seek to match themselves better with available work. In some cases they benefit by migrating to another area, where their skills are rarer and more valuable.

According to this view, then, firms demand labor only if the labor will increase the firm's profit level. Thus employers will want to hire workers who can produce well relative to the costs of hiring them. As economist Lester Thurow explains, "Firms simply rent individuals who possess the desired human capital assets just as they might rent physical capital. Individuals produce human capital assets because firms will rent them."[7] The employers' problem is to decide which worker will be the best bet. In some cases, such as the professions, a degree or credential is a requirement for job tenure. In crafts work, union apprenticeship is the key. Yet many jobs have no prerequisites: there are no schools for chicken gutting, ping pong ball manufacturing, or selling wire. Consequently, employers themselves provide the opportunity to develop workers' capital through on-the-job training. Their hope is that workers will develop an attachment to the firm as a result. Because training is costly, employers must have reason to believe the worker will be loyal and dependable.

Given this model of workers and employers, a simple explanation for inequality results. If women and minorities do poorly in the labor market, it must be because they have less human capital than white males. If hired, they can be expected to be less productive workers. So the rational employer will not place them to oversee the factory or control a multi-million-dollar budget.

The most commonly cited deficiency is education. It is claimed that children from poor families traditionally have had fewer supports to complete high school and go on to college. Minority children have sat in dilapidated school buildings with outdated texts, under the thumb of teachers more concerned with obedience than creative intellectual expression. Low education, the economists argue, implies poor work skills and attitudes. The cure for unemployment and low pay then is primarily more training programs, assisted by incentives to finish high school, and college scholarships.[8]

The very writers who pin inequality on education are strangely silent when it comes to the inferior economic position of women. If education were the key to good employment, then women and men should do equally well (discounting differences in years of experience). Except for professional education, girls sit in the same classrooms as boys, and are equally represented. Overall, girls take home better report cards. For these reasons, the human capital of females should be very good.

Rather than face the inconsistencies in human capital theory, advocates argue that women have deficiencies tied to sex. For example, they have, in the scientists' jargon, "low attachment to work" as a result of their devotion to hearth and home, spouse and offspring.[9] They are unreliable workers, who quit unexpectedly and take too many days off. At the same time, they are too devoted to their jobs, care little about advancement, and are geographically tied down. The scientists' message is clear: women have potential, but they don't give a damn about it. The solution, one that has seeped into much feminist rhetoric, is right in line with the cult of narcissism: For a woman to get ahead she must get her act together, from the right clothes to the correct attitude.

Minorities have also been accused of poor work orientation. For example, in his otherwise careful study of unemployment, economist Alan Sorkin concluded: "These findings strongly suggest that existing labor markets underutilize black workers and by discriminating against these individuals, prevent them from realizing their potential productivity. (However, *because their work habits may be less acceptable in comparison to those of whites* ... this conclusion should be accepted cautiously.)"[10] What is strange about Sorkin's afterthought is that nowhere did he look at work habits, so his offhanded caution, which can be refuted with other facts, defuses the impact of a major study identifying employers, not workers, as the cause of unemployment.

Another variation of human capital suggests that disadvantaged workers simply don't hitch their wagons to stars. They don't aspire to be eminent scientists, great politicians, major corporate executives, or outstanding artists. Without will, how can there be a way? This follows directly from the American Dream, with its belief that even little engines can make it if they try.

Through human capital theory vulgar ideas transubstantiate into the seemingly refined ones of science. While snickering at the popular view that women and blacks are dumb, lazy, or inept, social scientists explain rather that such workers are un-educated, unmotivated, and incapable of making the best use of themselves. If this is true, all we need do is redeem them—or cast them among the unworthy.

The theory's simplicity appeals to many. After all, if educa-tion or training are keeping certain people under, we can as a society pour more funds into that area for the long-term payoff of more productive workers, and subsequently, a higher Gross National Product. Thus it seems a more patriotic stand, and during the 1960s was the force behind the poverty policy.

The truth of the theory is another matter. Given its lack of precision, the nature of evidence required is unclear. Basically, it says that people of certain characteristics (women, minori-ties, presumably the disabled and older worker) are more likely to be ill-educated, wives, job quitters, or whatever, and consequently not do as well in the labor market. The theory doesn't say what deficiency carries more weight—say, poor training or little job experience. It also doesn't specify just what the casual chains look like. That is, does low education lead to unemployment, poor job opportunities, and low wages, or to just one of these forms of inequality? Given this lack of clarity in the framework, the numerous tests of this view form a col-lage, each cutting one scrap of reality. For the same semblance of order, we shall group the evidence with regard to the partic-ular outcome: finding employment, getting placed in a job of merit; and earning a liveable income.

Labor Participation

The most common question asked here concerns unemploy-ment and the role education and job commitment have in pro-

ducing it. Economists have long known that the more education a man, black or white, has, the more likely he will become
an employed worker. Only recently have researchers looked at
women as well, and they have come to a similar conclusion. In
fact, it is partly because of greater educational opportunities,
especially since 1940, that women have joined men on commuter buses and car pools.

But does low training explain the higher rates of unemployment among women and blacks? This used to be a reasonable
theory. In the early 1950s, for example, blacks had a median of
only 7.6 years of schooling, compared to 11.4 years for whites.
However, economists have observed that the gap between the
overall educational level of the employed and unemployed has
been narrowing since 1957. Educational equality is fast being
achieved in the United States. By the early 1970s, blacks had
12.0 years of schooling compared to 12.5 years for whites. Even
the proportion of white and black youth who have gone
through special vocational training is the same. So the differences in education for youth are not great enough to explain
why black teenagers have the enormously high rate of unemployment they do—ten to fifteen times that of white males.[11]

Thus, while education plays a role in overall unemployment,
it does not account for race and sex differences. That is, anyone
with only an eighth-grade education is taking many chances in
the labor market. But women and blacks do not have dispro-
portionate numbers of poorly educated workers, nowhere near
enough to explain their persistent difficulties in finding jobs or
landing positions free from the threat of layoffs. In other
words, many unemployed minorities resemble white males
who have jobs.

The other human capital factor that has been examined in
this regard is the female domestic role. For many years a common notion among sociologists has been that married women
do not work because to do so is to disturb family stability. It is
odd how persistently this claim has struck in the literature, because anyone who would bother to inspect labor force participation could see that married women have been taking on jobs
in increasing numbers. The greatest increase in recent years
has been the addition of wives with children under six years

old; fully one-third of this group work. Today over forty percent of married women work, as compared to only fourteen
percent in 1940. Hence being a wife or mother is no longer
keeping women from considering employment. These statistics
are readily accessible in census reports, a frequent and familiar
source of information to sociologists, who have nevertheless
preferred to maintain their comfortable myths rather than face
the facts.

Studies of employed wives indicate that they are likely to
seek paid labor, if anything, to enhance family stability. A wife
is especially prone to take a job under two conditions. One is if
her skills will attract a high salary. The college-educated wife is
more likely to work outside the home than the one with a
high-school diploma. The other condition is that her husband's
salary is low compared to other men in his occupation. So the
wife of a lawyer starting out in private practice will more likely
leave home in the mornings than one married to a partner in a
law firm. In view of these findings, we can see that being a wife
in itself does not inhibit employment.

Economist Jacob Mincer contends that women who wear
wedding bands are prone to higher unemployment for other
reasons.[12] Since married women are not the sole support of
their families, he argues, they are likely to be intermittent
workers, entering and leaving the labor force as the family
needs income. This theory makes sense at first reading. Unfortunately, Mincer's own research, which involves prolix statistical maneuvers, suffers serious technical flaws.[13] However, it
isn't necessary to be a highly trained statistician to check out
Mincer's idea. The unemployment data published monthly by
the government can tell us whether unemployed women are
disproportionately married. This is not the case. In recent years
the largest category of unemployed women have been married,
but their rate of unemployment is not much greater than that of
married men. The most vulnerable women economically—the
widowed, divorced, and separated—have a much higher rate of
unemployment than would be expected by chance. So even by
these crude indications, Mincer's idea fails to stand.

Finally, it is noteworthy that all human capital explanations
of unemployment miss an obvious point. Given that the popu-

lation survey counts as unemployed only those who have actively sought work the previous week, their count is prima-
facie proof that the people affected are not lazy or unmotivated.[14]

Occupational Discrimination

Scarcely any scientific research on this topic has been done
from a human capital perspective. This is odd, because the particular job one gets is the basis for wages, benefits, and other
rewards. But we know very little about how job choices and
searches are actually made by people in a day-to-day way.

One conclusion is clear: we cannot say that young white
males have higher job aspirations than other groups. In some
localities where research has been done this has proved true,
but in many others nonwhites or females were just as likely, in
some cases even more likely, to dream of becoming a doctor or
chemist or sports star.[15] Where the difference shows up is in *expectations*. Realistically, minority youth do not believe they have
as much of a chance as white youth to achieve their hopes. Most
teenage girls have career fantasies, but expect marriage will prevent their realization. Similarly, young blacks expect discrimination in education and hiring will preclude their success.

One test we can apply is to see whether schooling relates to
jobs.[16] For example, do all adult workers with one to three
years of college experience get similar jobs? We would expect
employers to value them for their advanced skills and high
motivation. However, the bulk of these workers who are female hold office jobs, where those who are male manage offices
or work in skilled trades. The men have a much greater range
of opportunities than the women. With regard to race, nonwhites with this much education are twice as likely as their
white classmates to end up in a factory or service establishment. Similar patterns of work segregation occur no matter
what level of schooling we investigate. What people look like
seems to matter more to employers than their competence.

In a curious way these data point out a paradox in human
capital theory with regard to women. Namely, women may end

up as secretaries for the very fact that they have invested time to learn typing and related skills. (The same holds true for nursing and teaching.) The better men's jobs—excluding the professions—require on-the-job training, and presumably employers use a diploma or evidence of college training in selecting candidates for these jobs. There is no reason why a woman *with* secretarial skills is less qualified for management training or crafts apprenticeship than a man *without* them. If anything, the fact that she has acquired the skills testifies to her general educability. The hitch is that an employer would rather put trained women in clerical jobs because doing so cuts back on his on-the-job training costs—he has an entire tier of positions for which he can forego special instructional costs. But in the process he may lose many persons who are exceptionally talented for other jobs. Thus to invest in one's human capital, for women, can mean increased discrimination, not less.

Wage Discrimination

The most sophisticated and careful test of the human capital approach has been the study of pay differences. Until a few years ago, those interested in the study of success looked only at men, often white men. Their explanation, still found in textbooks and papers on "manpower," is that adult white males are the "core labor force," the most important group, while women and minorities are "secondary labor."

In one typical study where investigators asked how it was that some white men were more successful than others, they found that the best predictors of success were a man's education and his father's social standing.[17] These two factors are the expressions of competing forces in the United States. The conservative force holds men to selecting jobs appropriate to the class into which they are born. The liberal force directs people to jobs equivalent to their skill or training. Of course, the two are related—it is easier to obtain advanced training if your father is an insurance company vice-president than it is if he is a sanding-machine operator in a furniture factory. Because schooling is not equally distributed in our society, it does not provide as broad a path to advancement as many people think.

Since this research was looking at the kinds of jobs men achieved, it did not often consider income, because it is common knowledge that certain occupations earn more than others. Sheet metal work brings in more than grape picking. But once the investigators allowed women and nonwhites into their purview, they were nonplussed to find that their neat model of achievement collapsed. For example, the most common female occupation is considered white-collar—the secretary. This job pays on the average much less than male white-collar jobs, even less than many male unskilled laboring positions. These discrepancies have forced researchers to consider sources of wage differences.

One typical study took samples of the experienced civilian labor force in 1973.[18] In this group, women earned on the average $6942 less a year than men. The researchers asked to what extent family background, education, occupational prestige, hours at work per week, job experience, and age could account for the salary gap. In other words, this study provided a direct test of the human capital approach.

The theory did not hold up well. Consider these results:

- The human capital people would expect to find that a person's social background would make a difference in wages, presumably because the middle and upper classes inculcate the habits and attitudes preferred by employers. This was true somewhat for men, but not at all for women.
- They would predict that education would account for large differences in income. Each year of education was worth $559 for men, but only $213 for women. Investment in education pays off more for men.
- They would expect the work-related variables (hours-per-week and experience) to explain women's lower wages. In fact, only experience made a difference, and then in men's favor. A year of experience netted the male worker $472, the female $38. Thus men gained over *twelve times* the payoff for the same time investment as women workers.

Thus the human capital theory failed to be upheld in two important ways. First, while social background, education, and work experience proved profitable to male workers, these factors did not explain the size of men's wages as well as the theory predicts. Second, the gap in earnings between women and men could not be explained by personal worker investments. As the writers concluded, "Discrimination accounts for 84% [of the earnings gap] in 1973." In other words, women could not be blamed for their low salaries.

A study of blue-collar workers on the job in 1973 produced similar results.[19] The men earned about twice as much as the women—and these were all full-time workers. Here is what it was worth to men and women to develop their "human capital":

	Men	Women
Each year of school	$158	$ 88
Each year of vocational training	626	228
Total benefits of schooling	784	316

Now, it happens that these women had almost the same education as men—thus their lower income was not caused by lack of trying. In fact, *the educational differences could account for only about one hundred of the several thousand dollars differences in wages.*

A third study looked at important work-related variables as well as education.[20] Researchers took workers from three census years (1950, 1960, and 1970) to see how absenteeism and job seniority affected wages. Most importantly, this study also included the number of hours worked per week. Again the results were disappointing to the investigators. That women work fewer hours than the average man could account for only about 11 percent of their wage gap. Education and job seniority each counted another 9 percent. So two-thirds of the extra income men earned could not be traced to their being full-time employees or more loyal than women.

Studies of race differences have produced comparable results. For example, one investigator asked whether schooling was a source of the race earnings gap in the 1960 male work force.[21] The lower educational level of minorities could account for only 6 to 8 percent of the difference. The rest of the gap seemed to be a result of the job assignments given minorities and whites. Thus, he concluded, the main reason blacks earn less is not inferior education, but the fact that employers place them in inferior jobs.

Another investigation used a national sample of 1962 male workers.[22] Overall, whites earned $3790 more than blacks. In this case, the amount attributed to schooling differences was only $520, or about 14 percent of the gap. After conducting several similar studies, one economist concluded:

> *In all cases, differences in schooling account for approximately 10 percent of the earnings gap. Although young blacks are rapidly approaching young whites in terms of years of school, we should not expect this narrowing of the schooling gap to have a major effect on the earnings gap between blacks and whites.*[23]

So again, in the case of racial inequality, we find the theory has been discredited.

These studies ignore the possibility that if minorities have inferior education to whites, then a black and a white of the same level of schooling would not have the same level of skills. One rebuttal to this interpretation is that the largest study of schools to date, James S. Coleman's *Equality of Educational Opportunity*, found much less variation in school quality than had been expected.[24] And except for elite schools like Harvard or Stanford, it matters little where a college graduate's degree comes from. Finally, in a clever test of the educational quality thesis, economist Barbara Bergman deducted a year from blacks' actual educational level to see whether this would explain their lower wages.[25] For example, a black high school graduate was treated as though he had only eleven years of schooling and compared with white male dropouts. This manipulation made no difference—the whites still earned much more money.

The most thorough analysis of paths to success to date has been made by a team of Harvard researchers directed by sociologist Christopher Jencks.[26] They examined the results of five national surveys of 25- to 64-year-old men, along with six special-purpose samples, such as those of brothers or unusually talented persons, to find out "who gets ahead." Three possible causes included in the study were human capital variables: academic ability, personal habits and traits, and education. If employers were hiring and rewarding men for their productivity, these factors would be strong predictors of success. Two other causes dealt with privilege (family background) and discrimination (race). If the American Dream were operating according to plan, these influences should have little role in explaining achievement. Their results indicate that human capital variables play only a minor role in explaining why some men make more money than others.

Academic Ability.   Men with higher IQ scores earn more than those with lower scores. If one man's IQ is 115, while his brother's was 100, his income would be $11,700 to his brother's $10,000. However, men with higher IQs are more likely to come from wealthier families, have high career aspirations, and attend school longer. The researchers concluded: "If test scores measure 'merit,' our data offer no evidence that the U.S. has grown more 'meritocratic.' "

Personality.   The Harvard team explored the role of self-assessments, personal behavior, and teacher ratings to see if any particular character traits led to success. They found small influences. For example, young men who perceived themselves as leaders were found later to be higher up the ladder of success than those who hadn't seen themselves in such roles. Teacher ratings also had a minor, though perceptible predictive ability. Nonetheless, the team "found little support for the idea that any single personality trait is of critical importance in determining individual success." The man of the American Dream, the one employers claim to prefer, did not emerge from the surveys.

Education.   The results of this test reduce simply to the advice to "finish school, preferably finish college." Apparently a diploma in hand is what matters most to employers. A couple of years of college do not provide much gain over a high school diploma; it's the completion that counts.[27] Unfortunately, though high-school completion is almost universal these days, college attendance and completion is much affected by a student's family background and financial resources.

If the human capital variables do not account for men's success, what does? Family background, especially the occupation and income of the father, as well as race. If you know these characteristics of a young man, you can make a good guess as to his future occupational status, and a fair estimate of his future income.

Scientific investigations aside, we need only look at the income distributions of workers to see that the human capital view makes little sense. The men at the top twenty percent of the scale earn five times as much money as those at the bottom twenty. But their IQs are certainly not five times as great, nor have they five times as many years of school. It is doubtful they are five times as industrious, hard-working, and loyal to their job. They are, however, likely to have fathers who earned five times as much money. Inheritance matters.

The American Dream is patently false. If women and non-whites are earning less or working less it is not because they are less skilled or educated. To invest in one's self is to have no clear ticket to success. A white male who goes to college is much more likely to obtain a prestigious job and high salary than his female and black classmates. No wonder many accomplished and successful men become impatient with others—they fail to understand that the Horatio Alger game works for only their part of the population (and they started with loaded dice to begin with).

The human capital approach fails to explain economic inequality because it is based upon a model of privileged white male achievement. So long as researchers were studying only white men, their ideas seemed to be correct. Once they admitted minorities and women into the counts, the theory collapsed. It was a bad theory from the start, a veneration of the success ideology, however translated into obscure technical language.

The key to success is to pick the right family to be born into—one whose lineage includes many of Anglo-Saxon heritage, with a father (and better, mother too) who has a good job.

It helps further if your father provides a Y chromosome and you are born able-bodied. Later, if you are good at taking tests and complete college, your position will be secured. Most of us have already missed out on this surefire formula by the moment of birth.

If well-motivated, educated, and talented workers are being underutilized and poorly rewarded in our society, then the primary basis for success must rest beyond individual effort. This is not to deny the role of individuality altogether, for particular traits fit certain jobs. Teachers must be fearless speakers, and professional athletes must rise above daily pain. (But with the exception of the few jobs requiring genius or prodigy, these requirements can be learned by the average person.) Today, too few people with superior traits and talents are getting the jobs the American Dream promises. The hopeful fantasies of youth end in a nightmare.

Chapter 6

Separate
Tollroads

Once a policeman asked me if I liked school and I said sometimes I did and then he said I was wasting my time there, because you don't need a lot of reading and writing to pick up the crops, and if you get too much schooling, he said, you start getting too big for your shoes, and cause a lot of trouble, and then you'll end up in jail.

Sharecropper's child to Robert Coles,
Children of Crisis

The most common assumption economists and policy makers assert when they study labor problems is that individuals rationally calculate their occupational choices. Personality profiles in *People, Us,* and newspapers translate this into "Successful people know what they want and go for it." Interviews never quote a celebrity of average talent as saying, "It was just by exploiting every connection that I got here," or the business executive as noting, "Well, my grandfather founded the company that owns this one." No, the actor slaved years to develop her craft, the executive plodded his way up from grocery clerk to vice president (as a *Fortune* profile on a Safeway heir described). Nor does *Time* gossip about the industrious, loyal, astute teacher who never gets promoted to principal.

The model of success holds true for just a tiny segment of jobs—medicine, law, high corporate management, professional sports, the arts, all positions requiring an early commitment to lengthy training or apprenticeship. Rarely does someone who takes her first ballet lesson in her late teens become a professional dancer. Aspiring concert pianists cannot begin at twenty. Mathematical genius shows early or not at all.

In contrast, the vast sweep of jobs in our society require but a brief vocational education or on-the-job training, so that it is unnecessary for a youngster to forge an early commitment. He need not say, "I'm going to become a punch press operator (or cabinet maker, or microcircuit assembler)." He doesn't even know what these jobs are—certainly he never sees them on television.

If the economists were right, then someone would sit down with the student and say, "Here are all the opportunities ahead of you. Now sit down and weigh the best ones in light of the interests and skills you have or are willing to obtain, the local labor market, potential racial or sexual discrimination, your appearance, your access to transportation, and the life-style to which you aspire." What actually happens is that youngsters are systematically dissuaded from applying logic at all.

Often in interviews successful people will claim that they knew as children they were going to be special. Here they are reporting accurately, but they miss that all children have vague, romantic fantasies of glory.[1] As youngsters, boys aspire to the heroes they see in movies and television—astronauts, police, and athletes. As young teenagers, they are only slightly more realistic in their hopes, aiming toward athletics, medicine, or science, or auto repair work. Girls, both young and early adolescent, dream of being teachers, nurses, secretaries, and models; as many girls as boys also want to be doctors.

By senior year in high school, aspirations of many youth shift in response to pressures from family, peers, and teachers. Over two-thirds of the girls who wanted to be doctors drop their intentions. Girls also switch their preferences from personal service jobs toward office work. Ninety percent of the black males who had wished to be scientists change their minds, and orient instead to the military or physical labor. Only white males retain their high hopes.

What all these changes mean is that by the time of the first job search, many youngsters are not open to a rational, broad survey of the labor market. They have suppressed some interests and talents in order to present themselves as normal, unthreatening young women, Chicanos, Orientals, blacks, or whatever. They accept society's view that they are unfit for many kinds of work.

COUNSELOR'S CHOICE

A standard resource for an adolescent is the counseling or career development office in high schools, junior colleges, and universities. In ideal terms, society charges the guidance counselor to direct a youngster toward the job that will most fit his or her talents, interests, and motivation. Since the labor market is so complex, counselors are supposed to navigate youth along the road map to various work locations. The reality of the situation is quite different.

Guidance experts learn about their jobs the way I became a sociologist, by reading about society instead of experiencing it. Instead of going out into the world and seeing how people work, observing real job interviews, and asking workers what they think about their lives, aspiring counselors attend classes taught by university professors in which most of the information comes from the work of yet other university professors. (It is no accident that such masterpieces as *Working* or *Labor and Monopoly Capital* were not written by academic specialists of labor.)[2] Students don't see smelters, mortuaries, auto parts warehouses, lumber mills, or insurance claims offices. They learn much more about how to fit people to jobs than about what the jobs are like.

Guidance counselors' own experience as job holders being atypical, they are hampererd from appreciating the pressures of garden variety work. They apply to school systems, where they work a ten-month year, and as semiprofessionals enjoy more job autonomy than is possible in other labor. Unlike most workers, who are vulnerable to evaluation throughout the year, counselors serve securely on annual contracts. They work inside and experience little physical exertion beyond the pulling of a file drawer. Guidance counseling has much to recommend it as a clean, meaningful, respected job.

Although counselors are supposed to have expertise in the composition of the job market and its changes, their sources of information are incomplete. The volumes of career guidance material aimed at high-school and college youth offer information so general that it is virtually useless in particular cases. Labor markets are much influenced by regional characteristics; it is silly for a North Dakota schoolboy to consider logging unless he is willing to move hundreds of miles. And as the aerospace engineers discovered, demand for a job can suddenly drop beyond any expert's expectations.

Even if a student explored the guidance materials and asked thoughtful questions, she would likely find blank spaces in place of answers. Although the government publishes thousands of statistics on income, educational requirements, job safety, unionization, and other work-related matters, different agencies collect the data, so no consistent comparisons of jobs can be drawn up. If an expert acquainted with this material cannot locate the basic characteristics of work in America, then how can we expect adolescents or job changers, even with expert help, to say, "I have looked the scene over, and in five years I'm going to be a class-one excavation machine operator earning $1500 a month."

Rather than guide youngsters, counselors assist schools by assigning students to different programs or encouraging them to pursue further education after graduation. Their major assorting device is the diagnostic test: "intelligence" forms that purport to measure students' aptitudes, and vocational interest inventories that claim to make a rational match of personality inclination to job.

The biases of IQ tests have been well documented.[3] Their wording and content favors the performance of middle-class students from verbally sophisticated families. Students who grow up in areas segregated by race, ethnicity, or class have different everyday experiences than the tests allow. The content of questions emphasizes the cultured, middle-class life, not the urban activities of working-class youth. Troubled by the need to feed and clothe their children, poorer parents have little time and resources to instill the methods of problem-solving that the tests emphasize. Researchers have been able to take children from poor families and train them well enough to raise their IQ by many points.[4]

Although such biases have been well publicized, tests continue to carry considerable weight in counseling decisions. In many schools, a single IQ test result is enough to classify a student permanently as a slow learner. The experts confuse ignorance with stupidity, and direct the lower-scoring children to programs providing little skill; they mistake experience for brilliance and push high-scoring children toward elite jobs. The tests are not used to diagnose strengths and weaknesses; they serve instead as a "scientific" device for giving out privileges. And somehow the children who had privileges to begin with end up with more at the end of the test session.[5]

The vocational interest inventories err in similar ways.[6] If a child has never known a white-collar worker and had little exposure to verbal activities, then how can she become interested in a managerial job? Interest generally follows, not precedes, participation. We grow fascinated with an activity after we've tried it, when we've thrown out the fantasy and based our enjoyment on experience. But interest tests presume that all students have had a wide range of opportunities. Surely young women are not going to show interest in skilled trades when they have no idea what carpentry or plumbing involves aside from "dirty work." With few exceptions, the inventories are also scored with an explicit sex bias. That is, a boy and a girl who mention the same interests will be directed toward different careers—ones that are considered suitable to their sex.

In other words, what seems to be a rational application of science through the technology of testing in fact fosters irrational, undemocratic, and exploitative results. The test-makers, who compete for millions of dollars in contracts every year, would have us believe they are sorting people out by merit. The counselors and school systems would be more honest if they just said, "Look, let's give all women, blacks, Italian-Americans, and other people from troubled families the minimal education, preferably one with a low-level skill that will get them a job but take them nowhere. Then let's take all the students with vocal, powerful, or affluent parents and give them the skills and attitudes they need to run the country's institutions."

It would be surprising if the counselors and teachers, as products of our segregated society, acted in any other way.

From their perspective, their actions probably seem eminently fair. Why shouldn't the students who do best on tests be pushed toward success? (No matter that the tests are poor predictors of labor behavior.) Why should poor students have their hopes raised when they could get along with less financial strain by going into a technical program? (No matter that the technical skill is outmoded in five years.) Why should a young girl be told to consider a course in mechanical drawing, when she'll only be embarrassed by the comments of the boys in the class? (No matter that this opportunity might spark a real talent.) Behind a veneer of humanity, misguided by testing technology, the well-meaning guides contribute to the destruction of lives.

HAPPENSTANCE AND CIRCUMSTANCE

By the time education is completed, most students do not have the training for a particular job. Those that do, such as secretarial students, have a wide range of employers to choose from. How do they decide just where to work? As far as we can tell, the choice is much the result of accident, little resembling the rational weighing of alternatives posted by economists in their labor market models.[7]

Consider what people say when you ask them how they got into their line of work. One boy's uncle was a plumber, so he got into the union apprenticeship program, while his best friend, who wanted to do the same, lacked a family connection and ended up at the meatpacking plant down the street. A girl went to a nearby insurance firm because her parents told her it was a respectable place for a young lady. An Oriental woman found piece work at the blouse factory in her neighborhood, because that's where all her relatives worked. A white male liberal arts graduate interviewed for management training positions, although he admitted he hadn't the slightest idea what a manager did. A woman college senior applied to graduate school because she couldn't type, and that was the major skill corporate interviewers seemed to want. (This last case was my own.)

The rationalist assumption also fails to make a time specification. A job seeker may decide wisely in terms of the short-run, though foolishly in terms of the long run. Perhaps one reason so many young women acquire clerical skills in high school is the fact that a job will then await them somewhere. Friends and family will say such a girl is "sensible" or "has her act together." However, clerical work in most firms is low-paying and offers little chance for advancement. What is an adequate salary in the first two or three years of adulthood will be scanty in the late twenties. Were young women told the long-term consequences of their investments, they might not be so quick to make them.

The view is even more confused by the fact that training programs in existence are seldom fitted well to societal needs. Though many fields in academia are glutted, the universities continue to spew out Ph.D.'s. While many more doctors are needed in rural and isolated areas of the country, the medical profession persists in limiting its classes so as to retain the advantages of scarcity. Few schools of education have followed Harvard's surprisingly radical decision to train not classroom teachers, but educational researchers and other support personnel. Similarly, vocational programs persist that teach techniques so outmoded or in such low demand that the student would do better to spend the time on a job where the skills acquired would be up to date. (The most recent example here is that of the computer schools, which charge several thousand dollars to teach skills that many companies gladly provide to promising employees.) The fact that a training school exists does not mean work is available once the certificate is in hand. Teachers, professionals, and technical-training personnel have vested interests in their own job, after all.

The traditional model of labor markets also assumes that individual workers sell their skills through a bidding process, one which ultimately results in an equilibrium where both workers and employers are satisfied with what they get. Some economists argue that workers compete for wages, while others argue that they compete for specific jobs. Either view imagines a line of potential workers with various capabilities being looked over by employers who match skills to needs and offer a wage in exchange. Football drafts follow this framework.

Economist Lester Thurow has offered his colleagues elegant and convincing technical explanations as to why this framework is inaccurate.[8] But it does not take economic sophistication to see its errors. On graduation day, the personnel directors of local companies do not go to the commencement activities to bid for workers, nor do we find them at the unemployment offices, eagerly competing for motivated employees. Rather, the workers go to the jobs; the most common method of job search is that in which applicants seek out employers on their own, one by one.

There are many communities that may harbor hundreds of potential employers. How can someone choose from such apparent richness? The answer is that the wealth is deceptive. Since no centralized labor directories or centers are available, applicants can uncover only a sampling of the firms in the marketplace. That information is likely to come from kin or friends. Since much of our society is residentially segregated by class, ethnicity, and race, individuals in one part of the locality will have a very different view of the job market than those in another neighborhood. This accounts for some of the homogeneity of workers in some jobs, for example, the many blacks working in the dry cleaning industry, or the Eastern Europeans in the steel mills. These like-groupings are reminders of the guilds of several centuries ago, where craftsworkers lived and marketed their goods in the same streets, the tin-goods makers here, the leather workers there.

Thus, in a society rife with competition and divisiveness, which requires its members to jockey constantly for good judgments in their comparisons with others, people seek the solace of working with those like themselves. And in fulfilling this need, they unwittingly ensure that segregated patterns continue.

Outside of friends and kin, potential workers turn to want ads and agencies as guides in their hunt. One recent study found that over three-fourths of the firms in Salt Lake City and San Francisco—cities with dissimilar labor markets—did not hire a single employee through the want ads in an entire year.[9] So workers who use this device eliminate the bulk of opportunities. A nationwide survey of job seekers in 1975 corroborated this conclusion. Only 15 percent of the women and 10 percent of the men located their job through the newspapers.[10] Fully one-third of workers simply went to a firm and filed an application, and about a fourth asked friends and relatives to recommend an employer.

Agencies are even less helpful than newspapers.[11] While employment agencies are supposed to provide a marketplace for worker and employer, they function to perpetuate work inequalities. Public agencies generally get only low-level jobs for their listings, hence they serve only the poorer members of the public. They provide a tax-paid subsidy to employers who do not have fulfilling, financially rewarding jobs, or who provide primarily seasonal or part-time work.

As laid-off aerospace engineers and teachers have learned, the public agencies have few referrals available to highly skilled workers. These must turn instead to private agencies. Although no detailed, wide-scale study of these organizations has been done, scattered evidence points to a history of abuses. Until recently outlawed, agencies and employers colluded in fee-splitting. The agency would send over a fee-paying client for unskilled labor, and the employer would soon fire or lay off the new worker. Abuses that continue today include purposeful misrepresentation of jobs in ads (for example, by implying that a secretarial job is really a managerial one) and persuasion of applicants to take jobs below their qualifications and interests.

The most persistent documented abuse remains discrimination. In one survey of 457 private agencies in eight American cities, investigators from the Anti-Defamation League posed as an employer who wanted a "white Gentile" secretary. Almost nine out of ten firms accepted the listing, often volunteering "We don't place colored" or "White Gentiles are always the most capable." Half of the agents who rejected the application—a mere five percent of all contacted—cited the law. When the ADL made the same discriminatory request of state agencies, not one accepted the order.

What we find, then, is that agencies sort out workers just as schools sort out students. Public agencies obey the laws, but place workers equitably among the low-level jobs they have on

file. Private agencies control the best work and distribute it unfairly.

Often overlooked in the discussion of work discrimination is
the question of the ease with which people within a community
can get to the jobs. Los Angeles provides a typical case of how
transportation networks can inhibit free access to labor markets. People who cannot afford cars or who own undependable
autos are left with only a mediocre municipal bus system to get
them around that sprawling city. The routes of this system
allow women from East Los Angeles or Watts to get to Beverly
Hills and other wealthy areas to work as maids, but do not let
their brothers and husbands travel directly to major industrial
areas.[12] A company can do all the community outreach it
wants, but if the transportation cannot get people to the factory, its efforts will not produce more equality.

Of course, a company with sufficient funds or mobility can
also move to be available to a cheap labor force. In recent
years, companies have located in the suburbs to gain the advantage of women workers who will work for less than their
sisters in the city.

By relying upon an informal word-of-mouth system for getting workers, employers can avoid accusations of discrimination. (This is why the federal guideline emphasizes the need for
firms to go into minority areas and publicize in minority
media.) They can ensure a homogeneity of work force, which
they believe is easier to control. They can locate part of their
production near the unemployed, be they poor or women
(often both), and gain from hiring such workers at low pay. But
they do so with the likelihood of losing some talented, committed workers, and the creative payoff that would result from
a more heterogeneous work force. American employers prefer
to sacrifice innovation and efficiency in favor of internal control
of employees.

Overall, the lack of a genuinely open labor market ensures
that potential workers of different backgrounds will find themselves in different jobs. The attitudes of counselors and parents, the street knowledge of friends, the availability of transportation, and the sifting activities of agencies conspire to
ensure that workers will end up in jobs that relate more to the

basis of their external appearance than to their intrinsic abilities.

SEGREGATED LABOR

The American Dream rings true because it has so much good sensibility to it. In a society starting fresh, say, on a desert island, the Dream could inspire a most humane community, one in which there would be some differences in the disbursement of rewards that would reflect both effort and contribution to the society. The more clever, adept, industrious fisher would draw more in trade than the one who preferred watching birds. In time, members of the society would recognize that the bird watcher had special talents (such as patience) well suited to other work (perhaps guarding the community), and would pay her accordingly for her usefulness. Rather than be ridiculed, the dwarf would earn appreciation for the fine tasks his body performed well.

Many small communities around the world distribute and reward labor according to these principles. While there may be rich and poor in these societies, the differences are a matter of the ownership of unusual shells and feathers, not in conditions that produce starvation, ill-habitation, and debasement of the soul.

We have seen how in its earliest years the United States ordered communities to respect and reward the special contribution of each adult. Survival in the New World demanded a contribution from everyone, able-bodied or not. But the cities brought wealth for a few; slavery grounded the privilege of race; industrialization forced the men from the home. The legacy of these conditions is a labor market in which workers are penned off from one another and kept with people of their own appearance and background. Affirmative action threatens because it insists that the fences come down, and workers be judged truly on their merits.

Where the guiding principle of residential segregation has been race and class, that of the work place has been sex. Many industries in our society are male-oriented, particularly those concerned with raw materials, basic manufacturing, and wholesale trade. For example, the following are just a sampling of current firms in which over 80 percent of the employees are male: mining, forestry, construction, wood products, dairy products, beverage industries, chemical production, transportation, utilities, auto repair, detective services. Women predominate among only seven types of firms: clothing production, private household labor, lodging homes, beauty shops, dressmaking shops, convalescent institutions, and libraries. This means that a male job seeker has many more employers receptive to hiring him than a woman does.

Jobs in our society are similarly sex-typed. Currently, 90 specific jobs are held almost entirely by men. These include architects, sales managers, earth drillers, carpet installers, fork lift operators, and fire fighters. When one looks at the male work force overall, this means that fully half of the men in our society have only men as their work colleagues.

Many fewer jobs are female-dominant (for example, nurse, child care worker, secretary, bank teller), yet one in three women work in these jobs. Thus the average employed woman has a much shorter list of job possibilities if she goes by word of mouth or personal observation.

In other words, two chunks of the labor market are fenced off "for men only" and "for women only" as clearly as the racial signs that used to hang on Southern public toilet facilities. Now, while I have checked the statistics on these statements and can show more precise figures to anyone,[13] I have known since girlhood that the world of work in our society was laid out this way. Yet the economists and policy makers continue to talk about a job market with open competition and blame women for being weak competitors. The wonder is that the public has let them speak so foolishly for so long in light of so much contrary evidence.

Though less visible, color bars also exist.

Since women make up half the work force, it is clear that something is wrong when 100% of all legal secretaries are women and 100% of all airline pilots are men. Statistically the possibility of an all-female or all-male occupation is more likely than that of an occupation made up of all one race. Comprising twelve percent of the population, blacks, our largest racial minority, have a plurality in only one job, paid domestic work. Still, one finds twice as many blacks as would be expected staffing the welfare office bureaucracies, mopping company floors in the middle of the night, and sorting mail.

Though no firm could be labelled "for blacks only," some are certainly "reserved for whites," especially those dealing with moneyed customers. The clerks in your hardware, clothing, bakery, and drug stores, the persons pumping your gas, the advisors in your security and investment offices, the professionals and their assistants in your dental and legal offices, all will have bleached faces—unless, of course, you are dealing with a business in a racially-segregated area. It has been a longtime practice in retail trade to place nonwhites behind the scenes, in the stockrooms, and not at the counters where white customers would have the embarrassment of dealing with them.

Turning to job categories, we saw in the third chapter that nonwhites seldom hold professional, technical, skilled crafts, and management positions. So the young Chicano or black woman sees no one leave the neighborhood in the morning to work as an industrial engineer, carpenter, social scientist, airline mechanic, or architect. It matters little that these occupations are becoming more open than in the past. The models are not there, and few young people have the courage of a Rosa Parks, to stand up alone and demand one's place.

HIDDEN INJURIES

The fence posts for these segregated labor markets were set by a variety of historical conditions. The cultures of slavery and patriarchy marked off large corrals. Laws established explicitly to keep blacks out, or to "protect" women from work that would have paid better, formed strong crossties. Labor unions reinforced the pattern with their exclusionary practices. Men, who benefited from the free household labor of women, set up

barbed wire to make the few women's jobs available look as unappealing as possible to other men. Employers wishing to defuse the grievances of workers threatened to tear down some of the fence and let "those people" into the mainstream. White male workers, many of whom hold jobs of little meaning and value, compensate by guarding their domain and looking down on the others.

Sex segregation in particular so profoundly shapes the lives of workers that when a woman and a man of the same background talk about their respective job problems, they have a difficult time understanding each other. Professional, managerial, and crafts jobs grant the most income, power, and prestige, gained at the expense of a lengthy apprenticeship. These positions bring with them the problems of deciding how to manipulate tasks, machines, budgets, and other workers. The psychic pressures of the powerful seem envious difficulties to the disenfranchised. These are also the problems of men. Over half of white men and a third of minority men currently enjoy the rewards and endure the responsibilities of these jobs, while less than a fifth of women do so.

Men in turn view women's work with distaste—the work of serving other people in beauty shops, libraries, offices, stores, and homes. Over half of all women take orders from other people, compared to less than a fourth of men. The most outstanding characteristic of this labor is low pay, which, in its extreme form, means no pay at all for housewives. Occupations that have large proportions of women bring in considerably less money on the average than those that are mixed or all-male.[14] When an occupation changes its sex composition over the years (though few have done so), the pay scales rise or fall accordingly. The entry of large numbers of men into elementary school teaching was quickly followed by an upgrading in that profession's financial reward and benefits.

None of the historical reasons commonly given for women's low wages apply in the seventies.[15] Today's new woman worker is likely to work throughout her adulthood, just like her brother. She is a stable worker—no more likely to be absent or quit. She is well educated. Her main reason for working

is the same as that for men: to support herself and her family. Nonetheless, women are paid comparably less today than their mothers were.

The financial depreciation of women exacerbates poverty. The largest growing sector of poor are displaced homemakers—women left on their own after divorce or bereavement to face a job market in which the openings are few and the positions simple-minded for one who has spent years in the complex management of a household and children. Contrary to public belief, only one out of five women actually receive support from ex-husbands. The children in these families become disadvantaged overnight, their economic fates turned for the worse by a noneconomic, private tragedy. The only cure for this type of poverty is better work for women, and the support facilities, such as childcare, to ease their burden. Yet government policy makers continue to talk as though the only persons affected by unemployment were married men.

Other families hover around the edge of poverty, slipping in and out, because both adult workers are disadvantaged. The men, of poor background, nonwhite race, or some physical disability, work at marginal jobs, receiving wages that in an inflationary economy are insufficient to support a family. Their wives, even more poorly paid, do not earn enough to bring the family income up to a comfortable and stable level. Given the double discrimination, two full-time workers bring home one and one-quarter of the salary earned by a privileged white male. All that toil, to give their children a handicapped start in life. All that effort, unappreciated by the affluent, to avoid the dole.

Society punishes disadvantaged workers psychologically as well as economically.[16] Women's work incurs daily psychic pain, erodes self-respect and confidence. In bureaucracies, women clerks must be punctual, take lunch and rest breaks at appointed times, and cannot do work outside the office; male supervisors can come and go as they please, work in restaurants or on tennis courts. In stores, women clerks must look busy and not talk to one another, while men can stand in clusters and "chat about business." Women serve as the organizational blame-takers—the ones customers complain to about decisions made by managers. Secretaries are to be loyal to their bosses, to the point of illegal and unethical behavior. Women are not to complain if a male employee or client acts in a sexually harassing manner.[17]

Examples abound that demonstrate how the position of women at work mirrors the privileged man's view of her proper role in life. She is to work hard, uncomplainingly, smiling and deferrent, with all the virtues of the American Dream and none of its rewards. The process repeats itself in similar form with other disadvantaged people. For example, a young working-class white man, discouraged by school, takes unskilled laboring jobs that buy a flashy car for a bachelor, yet barely house and feed a young family several years later.[18] He works in dangerous, dirty, and uncomfortable places, while nightly he watches men in suits at their well-paying, adventuresome jobs. He exhausts himself moonlighting or in overtime to give his family the best, which in the end is merely adequate. He says "sir" to men in banks or government offices. His job brands him as a loser, and he does not consider that he loses so that others can win. He wants to win too.

Society is not satisfied that people slip into the cloaks of their appropriate work and earn their rewards accordingly. It demands that they capitulate their minds as well, internalize a destructive self-deception. A secretary tells a friend how lucky she is to work in an attractive office, and ignores how much more appealing the off-limits executive areas are. A young woman with cerebral palsy smiles into the television camera and exclaims how grateful she is to hold a job in a sheltered workshop at a dollar an hour. An articulate middle-aged blue-collar man in a bar damns himself for not having any more brains, oblivious to the fact that no one gave his mind a chance. A young black man, employed for the first time eight months after high-school graduation as a stock clerk earning minimum wages, eagerly labors, grateful to his employers, certain that he will rise to become manager of a drug store run by one of the most racially-discriminatory chains in the city.[19]

These lives, these personal troubles, are the casualties of the

American Dream ideology. They comprise the majority of workers in the country. Yet because they are corralled into different pens, they fail to see that they share the same fate, that their fences are all of one making.

Chapter 7

Craven Gatekeepers

It is a distinct disservice to [blacks] to admit them to schools where they cannot succeed, and where their poor performance confirms rather than dispels the false stereotypes about minority abilities.

> Committee on Academic Nondiscrimination
> and Integrity, Amicus brief,
> U.S. Supreme Court, Bakke

Since there are virtually no black scientists in the United States, there is little opportunity, even if the predisposition were present, for the scientific community to consciously deny black scientists high social position.

> Jonathan and Stephen Cole,
> Social Stratification in Science

In the American Dream, employers look over workers, decide whether they are qualified, and choose to hire them. This was true when the economy depended upon small shops, crafts, and farms to supply most goods. Once industrialization brought the need for large numbers of workers in one factory, agents played a major role in acquiring labor. These agents were in effect subcontractors for the employers and followed their wishes. As the work force increased in skill, employers came to depend more upon individual applicants, especially as referrals from other employees as a source of new labor.

However, the choice of workers is not in the employers' hands for elite jobs in both blue-collar and white-collar occupations. A hospital administrator cannot independently decide who is competent to perform a doctor's duties (for example, a highly skilled nurse), but must hire an M.D., certified by the medical profession itself. In the crafts, science, law, medicine, academia, and similar occupations, worker organizations control entry into training and often into the first job.

It is worth examining these groups in detail for several reasons. First, though their social histories are different, their current behavior toward women and minorities is similar. Second, as elite workers, other occupational groups look to their practices and adopt them. Finally, they employ similar practices to exclude some Americans from their groups, and to limit the achievement of those disfavored who manage to get entry.

UNION HYPOCRISY

Soon after the Liberty Bell rang out for national independence, workers organized to improve their laboring conditions. "Equality of opportunity" was the motto of many groups, such as the Mechanics Union of Trade Associations of Philadelphia. Up until the 1880s, union issues were often social issues. The Knights of Labor enrolled all kinds of people—skilled and unskilled, women, blacks, even farmers—into its assemblies. These groups pushed for child labor laws, immigration control, and the abolition of prison labor, among other broad policies.

Competing views developed after the Civil War. The first large-scale exclusion of blacks by a private organization was undertaken by the National Labor Union, which in 1869 asked nonwhite members to separate and form their own organizations. (That same year the Knights of Labor set a policy to secure for both sexes equal pay for equal work.) Crafts unions, which organized around one skill rather than many, were the defensive response of white males of native stock, who felt little identity with foreign-born workers of differing ethnic or religious background, and feared their entry into the marketplace.

In 1890, the social issues contingent seemed to win out, when it convinced the American Federation of Labor to refuse membership to the racially discriminatory National Association of Machinists. Leader Samuel Gompers said that workers "may not care to socially meet colored people, but as working men we are not justified in refusing them the right of the opportunity to organize them for their common protection."[1]

Gompers soon changed his tune. In 1895 he capitulated to the demands of crafts unions and admitted the Machinists to membership. He supported writings of the AFL organizer who wrote: "It was a fact to every observing man who has studied the Negro from contact that as a race, he does not give evidence of possession of those peculiarities of temperament, such as patriotism, sympathy, sacrifice, etc., which are peculiar to most of the Caucasian race."[2] Gompers' compromise was to allow blacks to form separate locals, a practice that persisted until the 1960s in many areas of the country.

By 1900, the exclusionary crafts unions dominated the AFL. Young black men whose fathers had engineered trains and carved mahogany banisters in mansions found themselves unable to ply their trades. The organization also participated in attempts to stop immigration by arguing that a "loss in racial purity and strength" would ensue.[3]

The foreign born were both denied advantages and scorned for being without them. For years Irish, Italians, Hungarians, Poles, and others were called shiftless, dirty, and dull-minded. Only the hardest laboring work was permitted them, mining in the bowels of the earth, or producing steel in the ovens of the smelters, where they were in effect forced labor, subject to starvation wages and menial treatment. The crafts unions refused to accept these workers.

Except for textile and clothing workers, most employed women were not active in union affairs at this time. Rather, political activists such as Emma Goldman, Jane Addams, and Mother Jones fought for the improvement of working conditions for all, and the anonymous wives, sisters, and daughters of many union men fought on picket lines and streets. The men did not repay the ladies' valor by opening up jobs or including the bulk of employed women into their organizations.[4]

In the 1920s the AFL garnered further support from members for its racist ways when industries such as steel purposely hired blacks as strikebreakers. By this time the unions functioned like guilds, as hereditary groups. They gave a small edge to white laboring men, one earned through decades of strife and bloodshed. (During this time employers were outbuying enforcement agencies in the purchase of tear gas, ammunition, and guns.)[5] Today it is easy to forget that the eight-hour day, overtime pay, and clean work places are recent features of an employee's life, won much from the courage, persistence, and sacrifice of strikers and their families. Seen in this light, it is understandable, if not morally defensible, that a man would seek to control his craft, and thus be able to pass on to his son the birthright to a protected job.

Eventually, several wise labor leaders revitalized the broader social emphasis of earlier days. Thus, in 1935, when the AFL refused to hold hearings on the problems of black workers or to consider the organization of women and ethnic white labor as well, John L. Lewis and colleagues formed the Committee for Industrial Organization.[6] The CIO constitution barred no one from membership because of "sex, race, creed, or national origin." The CIO creed was not rhetoric. In just a few years thousands of black men and men of Eastern and Southern European origin, long excluded from membership, carried union signs at demonstrations; thousands of women held cards in such mass industrial unions as the electrical workers, packers, and assembly workers.

When the AFL-CIO merged in 1955, Walter Reuther said to the founding convention, "I believe that this labor movement of ours will make a great contribution in the field of civil liberties and civil rights."[7] The union leaders took Reuther seriously, by filing complaints against affiliates, negotiating antidiscrimination clauses, and urging the formation of civil rights committees. Yet a 1961 study by the NAACP concluded that most actions had been ineffective. The Ku Klux Klan and White Citizens Council continued to influence Southern locals. When A. Philip Randolph, president of the black Brotherhood of Sleeping Car Porters vocally criticized the unions, the AFL-CIO council chastised him publicly for making "unfair and untrue allegations."

Recent examination of union activity has proven Randolph right. Since the introduction of the 1964 Civil Rights Act, the position of blacks in unions has not improved.[8] In 1969 they comprised 1.9 percent of unionized electrical workers, 2.7 percent of iron workers, 2.7 percent of operating engineers, 2.9 percent of carpenters, and about 25 percent of laborers. Scarcely any Asian-Americans have entered crafts unions; those who have, live in Hawaii.

In 1967, the U.S. Department of Labor announced that trade-union locals could face denial of federal certification if they did not admit nonwhites to the apprenticeship programs.

This threat was not implemented. A careful examination of 75 cases of racial discrimination complaints brought before the Equal Employment Opportunity Commission concluded that remediation efforts had almost no effect.[9] After months of negotiation between the EEOC and unions, only 18 agreed to any changes, most of which did not repair the systematic exclusion of minorities.

Except during World War II, women have filled few skilled crafts jobs (about 2 to 3 percent), and so have not even mattered in crafts union harangues.[10] The few female occupations that have been unionized—clothing construction, retail trade, teaching, communications work—have not been notably successful in meeting the special needs of female workers.[11] First, they are run by men, who fail to administer locals in a way that encourages worker participation. (For example, meetings are scheduled at night, when women are less willing or free to attend.)[12] Second, the jobs covered by union contracts tend to be ones in which little advancement is possible, so they do not provide the benefits and protections of the male union jobs. Third, in the past males obtained contract clauses to exclude women from better jobs, or to pay women less in the cases where they worked alongside men. Though these practices are now illegal, they have set up a pattern difficult to break.[13] In sum, union membership for women has offered little more than an extra deduction from the paycheck.

Although the Department of Labor has urged that 20 percent of apprenticeship and training programs in the crafts be open to women, only about 2 percent of recent classes have been female. In 1976, only 271 women *in the entire nation* were registered carpenter apprentices—less than one percent of all such apprentices. Similar figures were tallied for machinists, electricians, pipe fitters, and tool makers.[14] With so few women in training, the prospect of large numbers of women wearing hard hats in the 1980s is a feminist's fantasy.

A 1974 search of referral unions by the EEOC uncovered further facts which indicate that even those women and minorities who get into unions may not receive equal treatment.[15] Referral unions act as recruiters for employers. Construction company owners rely upon building trades to supply skilled

labor, be it bricklaying, elevator construction, or marble pol-
ishing. Nonbuilding firms that use referral are those needing
truck delivery, hotels and restaurants, movie houses, and some
service companies. Union members earn 20 to 25 percent more
in wages than comparable nonunion employees. Obviously,
discrimination at the union level will lead to the appearance of
discrimination at the employer's firm.

At first glance, it appears that minorities have signed into
more union hiring halls in recent years since the 1969 census
discussed above. But a closer inspection of specific union membership uncovers widespread bias. With the exception of
bricklaying, blacks are excluded from the best-paying construction trades, and have unusually high numbers in the low-
paying ones, such as roofing or general labor. Hispanics have a
better record, being found among sheet metal, electrical, or
iron workers, although again most are in the low-paying jobs.
Asian-Americans are virtually missing from all the rolls. Surprisingly, Native Americans are present in all construction jobs
at a much greater frequency than would be expected by
chance. As for women, little can be said because so few are on
construction sites—about one-fortieth the number one would
expect by chance.

The minorities fare better in the nonbuilding trades, though
again signs of bias are present. For example, while blacks and
Hispanics number well among teamsters, they pull the in-town
delivery or warehouse jobs, not the lucrative long hauls. They
seldom work in such skilled occupations as movie projection-
ist, pattern maker, or printer. Asian-Americans and Hispanics
are overrepresented in poorly-paying hotels, restaurants, and
garment factories. Women do not prosper in nonbuilding referral unions either. Minority women sew and clean clothes,
while white women wait at store counters or lunch tables.

The forecast for these groups in the next few decades is
mixed. Those trades where minorities are starting to do well
are also the very ones on the decline as construction methods
change. On the other hand, skilled carpenters, bricklayers,
plumbers, and such already exist throughout the minorities, so
if unions accepted these talented workers, their incomes would
rise appreciably.

The possibilities for women's advance in the better-skilled referral unions are simply nonexistent.

To conclude, large segments of organized labor remain exclusive, insular guilds that operate to give some workers an edge over others. This persistent discrimination is a blot upon a history of courage and honor.

MEDICINE: A DISEASED PROFESSION

Except for Supreme Court justices, doctors have the greatest prestige of any job in the United States.[16] Part of this recognition is due to the value Americans place upon techniques to avoid death, and to the lengthy, arcane training for medicine. But part too is a result of the profession's success in managing its own image, and most importantly, in controlling the size of its work force. By keeping the number of physicians in the country small and obtaining a political monopoly on health care, medical doctors have ensured for themselves lives with considerable autonomy over their jobs, control over large numbers of other health workers, and material riches unmatched by all but top executives and celebrities.

To have a child become a doctor or marry a doctor reflects upon the entire family, winning respect and establishing proof of the family's exceptional ability. Other jobs that require just as lengthy training, and in some cases, more intellectually demanding experiences, do not provide this glitter. (Everyone knows that biochemists, nuclear engineers, or experimental psychologists are not "doctors," even though they have degrees dubbing them so.) In fact, many occupations look to medicine as a model for their own practices, and presume that by adapting such features as licensure or a code of ethics (on paper if not in practice) they can gain more income and respect. Consequently the activities of that profession guide the lives of many other workers.

The history of the medical profession has been one of blatant and purposeful discrimination.[17] The first U.S. medical school, the University of Pennsylvania, barred women from its program when it opened in 1767. When Elizabeth Blackwell applied to Geneva Medical School in 1847, she was accepted as a joke. Harvard University accepted three blacks and one woman in 1850, but the other students rioted, forcing the newcomers to leave. In 1876, a black admitted to the University of Pennsylvania Medical School was allowed admission provided he sit behind a screen in the classroom.

The American Medical Association, the governing body for training and practice, first met in 1846 to establish the primacy of medicine over other healing approaches. Its formal decisions reinforced the actions of individual schools. In 1870 it debarred the black National Medical Society of Washington, ostensibly on the grounds of low educational standards, and removed two black hospitals from its approved list as well. In 1868 it tabled a discussion on admitting women members. When a woman surprised the convention with her attendance in 1876 (having registered in advance with her first initials), the membership voted to have its Judicial Council decide upon the admission of women. The council said yes—forty years later. The practice of giving preference to doctors' sons over the years also penalized those white men from families without professional connections.

Until recently, minorities and women who wished to become doctors had the best chance of meeting their goal either by attending segregated schools or by going out of the country. As late as 1950, one-third of all schools explicitly banned blacks. Consequently, most black physicians practicing today have degrees from Howard or Meharry. Others followed the path of Charles R. Drew, who received his degree from McGill in Canada and went to England to carry on his important work on blood plasma transfusion. (Ironically, Dr. Drew bled to death following an auto accident in North Carolina, when the nearest hospital, for whites, refused to admit him.)

Hispanics have gone to Mexico for training. When in the early 1970s Mexican-Americans found themselves excluded from medical training in this country, they appealed to the President of Mexico, who offered forty scholarships for study there, even though he knew the students would return to practice in the United States.[18] In California the state medical schools all totaled accepted only one Mexican-American in

1968. At present, almost all Hispanic doctors practicing in San Diego County were trained out of the country.

As of the late seventies, the number of blacks and Hispanics attending medical schools was only half as great as would be expected given their numbers in the population.[19] Asian-Americans were finding entry, probably because that ethnic group encourages scientific training. (During the early years at Davis Medical School, the only minorities accepted were Asian.) Similarly, only two-fifths as many women are getting into the classrooms as would be predicted under an equitable system.

Traditionally, medical schools have given favored treatment to people of privilege.[20] In 1973, John Silber, president of Boston University, said, "We don't admit someone to our Medical School or Law School who isn't qualified to get in, but at the same time when we facilitate that admission there's no reason why we shouldn't go right back to the person, the father of the person who's been admitted, and talk to him about a gift to the school."[21] That same year the Chicago Medical School admitted favoring 77 out of 91 applicants on whose behalf pledges of financial support were made. In 1976, the dean at Davis verified news reports that he had a few "special interest" slots which allowed him to place children of wealthy, powerful, or famous parents. A dean at a Pennsylvania school, Hahneman, said that half of all applications included letters from politicians, and that such pressures sometimes swayed committees. In San Francisco, the son of a powerful black newspaper owner was placed in a residency program above the veto of the faculty admissions committee.

If special interest admissions continue along with affirmative action, then a squeeze is placed upon applicants like Allan Bakke, those who are not members of recognized minorities, yet who lack the financial or political clout to favor their case. The U.S. Commission on Civil Rights has argued that white applicants did not lose as a result of affirmative action programs, because the size of the classes grew, with most of the seats going to whites.[22] But were these whites from working-class ethnic neighborhoods? Were they the children of postal clerks? Or were they sons and daughters of prominent and wealthy community members? The commission is silent on this point.

The profession's discrimination against women and minorities persists beyond medical school acceptance. One practice is to direct disadvantaged people toward the less prestigious, less well-paying specialties. For example, hardly any female doctors enter surgery, cardiology, or gastroenterology; they are even less likely than men to become gynecologists. Instead they end up in pediatrics (where else would a woman be a "natural"?), public health, preventive medicine, and anesthesiology.

The other discriminatory practice is to block the acceptance of immigrant doctors. In recent years the wave of Asian immigrants has included skilled, established health professionals. At a Civil Rights Commission hearing in 1974, witnesses testified that these doctors were being rejected by intern or residency programs and denied doctors' privileges at hospitals.[23] Some were hired as technicians or nurses' aides. Others were allowed to perform medical procedures, yet were paid less than nurses. The medical associations' explanation—that these doctors did not possess a Standard Certificate issued by the Educational Council for Foreign Medical Graduates—suggested the use of bureaucratic devices to disguise nefarious purposes. It seemed not to have occurred to them that the medical profession might find other means by which to test the competence of these talented individuals.

EFFETE SNOBBERY

The short history of affirmative action programs in medicine demonstrates their efficacy in affording opportunities to some of those students who would have been excluded in the past. Unfortunately, little evidence exists to show that other elite professions, particularly the academic ones, are as yet following medicine's lead, perfunctory though it be.

One reason why the medical schools had so few women and minorities for many years was not pure discrimination on their part, but a lack of applicants from undergraduate colleges. For blacks, Hispanics, and others, the door to college was a tight one that opened only sporadically to allow a few entries. For women, too, attendance was difficult, and those who attempted to explore scientific fields faced discouragement and even ridicule from counselors and faculty.

Scarcely any information exists on the status of minorities in the Ph.D. professions. This lack of knowledge matters little, however, because so few minorities enter Ph.D. programs in the first place. In 1971, only one out of one hundred graduate students in the country was black—a sorrier record than the medical record. Although no statistics are available on Hispanics or Native Americans, it is unlikely that they attend graduate schools in numbers appropriate to their population.

According to the most recent and comprehensive survey of all persons with doctorates, 6 of 100 with science degrees are minorities. They are most commonly found in computer science and engineering, fields where Asian-Americans have forced unusual success. Surprisingly, even fewer minorities hold humanities doctorates—3 of 100. Here they have better chances in music and the social science. Overall, they are uncommon sights in departments of psychology, earth science, art history, and English or American literature.

The sponsor of this study, the National Research Council, did not explore the role of minorities in any more detail than these figures indicate.[24] Given its data collection techniques, it could have disclosed which minorities were in what fields, the types of jobs they held, or the salaries they earned. But it didn't, and its neglect is suspect. The Council is supported by a collection of scientific organizations, and one wonders whether they simply didn't want to broadcast bad news.

Their information on women doctorates is more detailed. Females hold 10 of 100 science degrees and 22 of 100 in the humanities. More often they work in medical, biological, and psychological laboratories, or teach literature and languages; they are rare in engineering, physics, geology, and agricultural projects, or in philosophy and social science classrooms.

When salaries of women and men are compared for full-time workers, the women are often thousands of dollars behind. Men in science earn $26,000 to women's $21,000; men in the humanities earn $21,100 to women's $18,300. These differences hold whether the employer is business, government, or university.

In all fields men hold higher academic ranks. And women have three times the unemployment rate of men.

The National Research Council reported these findings without a single interpretation or comment. They were being "just scientists"—stating the facts, that's all. Yet facts like these, which sit on the desks of deans and university presidents around the country, have a way of becoming standards. Does the NRC mean to state that women as a state of nature earn $5000 less a year than men, just as the atomic weight of hydrogen is 1.00797?

Some scientists have come to the fore to explain why women fare badly.[25] Their answer is a familiar one—the human capital approach. It is argued that women have family demands keeping them from performing well. (Yet half of the women with doctorates are unmarried.) Others say the women don't publish enough, while ignoring the fact that they do not get jobs at the schools with research facilities or are given subordinate roles on projects. (We don't know how many women assistants write portions of papers the male directors claim as their own.) They claim women scientists are not motivated, while overlooking the enormous pressures these scientists overcame in this society even to earn a degree. Some suggest that because so many women doctorates are at schools with a primary commitment to teaching, the women are doing what they want to do, and this is why they are not productive. This ignores the fact that schools with research facilities are much less likely to hire women; in other words, if the women are full-time teachers it is not necessarily out of choice. Finally, some note that the work women publish is not as good as that published by men, since it is not cited in later studies. This explanation ignores the well-documented belief that women do not have anything of value to say. A paper must be read in the first place in order to be cited.

The apologists don't argue one point, that women scientists are less intelligent than men, because the evidence is that they are brighter. Then why aren't they winning more Nobel Prizes?

The social arrangements of big league academia are among the most feudal in our society. Professors vie on the fields of research grants and publishing. A prominent, successful academic requires a following of vassals and serfs to assist him—people to plod through the tedious collection of data, to draft reports and type projects. Also, someone has to teach the undergraduates. Graduate students and women fill these roles admirably. For male students, serving as an assistant is an apprenticeship; for women, it is practice in the job they will be expected to take throughout their careers.

Until recently, nepotism rules forbade academic spouses from holding regular jobs at the same institutions. Traditionally, the man would be hired, and a temporary or part-time job found for the woman—or she would search for a position at a smaller school nearby. Cases are on public record, and are well known in academic gossip, of wives who co-authored their spouse's work yet received no scientific acknowledgement. With so many obstacles to performance and recognition, it is no surprise that half of all academic women are unmarried. Unlike their male colleagues, they cannot have both a family life and fulfilling career.

Academics so far have failed to admit their discriminating practices, let alone recognize the virulent racist and sexist attitudes upon which they are based. In its most recent and pernicious form, neoconservatism purports that the presence of women and minorities in our universities is leading to deterioration in educational quality. A good example of this reasoning was the remark of a college dean, who, in describing the first years of open hiring on his faculty, bemoaned how the procedure lowered faculty quality. "Minorities, including now impatient women, used affirmative action to leap into positions of power or to retain their jobs. Minorities were underrepresented on the faculty, and one could scarcely contemplate dismissing a black, a Puerto Rican, or a woman unless he or she was utterly incompetent."[26] The implication, ironically unintentional, was that such workers could have been fired in the past even if they were competent. More obvious is the suggestion that the minorities and women, while hired by a prestigious college through a process filled with more checks and balances than most job hirings in this society, would somehow be incompetent. (If they were indeed inept, then one must question the wisdom of the white males who took them on in the first place.) However one veils the rhetoric, neoconservatives are really saying that women and other disadvantaged groups are dumb.

The consequences of academic discrimination are far reaching. Only white boys have models of intellectual leadership. When the only Hispanic faculty in a school are the teachers of Ethnic Studies, one can wrongly deduce that they lack the ability to teach anything else. When heads of government or business seek an academic for advice in policy matters, they will hear the perspective only of another privileged white male. In sharing the same position in society, the two may readily agree on the solution of a problem, but there is also a good chance it will be an utterly wrong solution because it overlooks the needs and preferences of other groups.

Since academics, scientists, and intellectuals create and reinforce the dominant values of their times, those values of service to privileged men get unequal due. Engineers design better rockets, not safer kitchens. Historians discuss war, not family life. Economists design full employment for men, not women. Literature courses prescribe Hemingway and Mailer, not Baldwin and Morrison. Our classrooms, from kindergarten to professional schools, preach not the rich diversity of cultural views that comprise the human wealth of this nation, but the narrow, self-serving attitudes of the powerful and wealthy.

Chapter 8

Feudalism in Disguise

The issue is not simply that most women are in a separate labor market. So are most men, but they're not complaining. The real issue is that the labor market women are in is unequal in a myriad of bread-and-butter ways.

Louise Kapp Howe, Pink Collar Workers

The greater the reserve army in proportion to the active labor-army, the greater is the mass of a consolidated surplus population, whose misery is in inverse ratio to its torment of labor.

Karl Marx, Das Kapital

If the American Dream were correct, then a capable and wise worker would not be deterred by a bad break in his first job. He would see discrimination at the time of employment as just one obstacle to be conquered on the way up. Economists and career development experts reinforce this belief by arguing that talented, hard-working people will float to the top of their career lines, to enjoy middle age with the rich satisfaction of a job that has both responsibilities and rewards.

Contrary to popular belief and the experts, jobs in the United States provide varying degrees of promise. Some are dead-end jobs, such as tossing hamburger patties at a fast food shop, though the workers who take these jobs are aware of the limitations. Other jobs promise so much prestige and payoff from the start, such as in medicine, that the question of advancement is almost irrelevant. Managerial jobs most closely resemble the success myth's model, for they allow the college graduate to move up through sales to marketing to a vice-presidency. Military organizations also follow this principle. But the bulk of jobs do not provide anything like the degree of advancement claimed for them by the optimistic career preachers.

Jobs do not exist in a vacuum. They are set firmly within organizations and segments of the economy, and their placement influences their shape and opportunity. When we look at the reality of job arrangements in the United States, we see why hard-working and talented people can lead empty lives in a struggle for basic needs.

HOW TO FAIL IN SPITE OF TRYING

In the Broadway musical *How to Succeed in Business without Really Trying,* J. Pierpont Finch moves himself from mail clerk to company president through guile and charm. The plot is a male Cinderella story. Where a woman succeeds by entrancing a prince, the male transforms himself into the prince. Finch occurs no more often in real life than Cinderella. It takes a princess to marry a prince, and the prince is a prince by birth. Most of us are vassals.

Finch's miraculous mobility posits a work organization that never existed in this country. When the population was smaller and less based upon industrial technology, owners personally employed and managed their work forces. The work-place atmosphere depended upon the mood and maturity of the boss, who could be a benevolent patriarch or a Scrooge. The unrelated worker had little hope of taking over the firm (unless he married the boss' daughter)—yet he could reasonably expect a secure and comfortable lifelong position.

As machines clanged methodically into the work places, owners required new methods of control to fit workers' behavior to the new rhythms.[1] New England woolen mills hired scores of young women from depressed rural areas, worked them fourteen hours a day, housed them, and regulated every minute of their lives, from prayer to play. The women had no expectation of spending their lives in the mill towns, so they were all of a class—equally tired, harassed, and underpaid. Young men flocking to the iron and steel mills fed the furnaces with only the bad luck of an accident for escape. A pig-iron hauler was fortunate to become a supervisor in his lifetime, let alone a Carnegie.

As the size of the work force and the complexity of production grew, owners had a new problem. They were running out of sons, brothers, and nephews to manage the new departments and subsidiaries. By virtue of blood and law, family members would be counted on for their loyalty and trustworthiness. But if the company outgrew the family, then it was necessary to locate other workers on principle to assist in the operations. The answer was to find men who looked and thought like family. This is why even today the managers of large companies resemble each other like cutouts from a book of white male Republican Episcopalian middle-aged models. They may not have been born princes, but they were born well enough to make a good imitation.

Furthermore, as the number of jobs within a firm increased, the owners found it useful to separate workers into different groups. No longer would the workers, united, struggle for their rights against the employer; instead, they would compete against one another. The employer found it to his advantage to plump up some jobs while leaving others scrawny and lean. Through this differentiation of labor, no worker had hopes of becoming a prince; however, some were allowed the appearance of nobility. The workers were broken into ranks against one another.[2]

To appreciate the reasons for these changes, imagine the problems of the owners of a large plant that produces a variety of goods. They will need production workers, secretaries, maintenance people, distribution people, a sales force, and management. For some jobs, such as that of plumber or nurse, they will have to depend upon a union or professional organization to set the initial qualifications for the work and provide applicants. For most others, however, they can devise their own requirements and specifications.

With the exception of special and widely transferable technical skills, such as typing, the bulk of the training will be on the job. Consequently, the skills required for a job are specific to that job within a particular enterprise. If the worker cannot take these skills to another company, why would she take the job in the first place? Because employers provide incentives in the form of benefits, promotions, and (after a probationary period) the promise of security. The employer benefits by getting a committed worker who is unlikely to leave, and the worker gains from the rewards she might not get in another, more transferable job.

Economists observe that on-the-job training prevails in blue-collar work, but a quick look at any office and many other settings will demonstrate that it occurs with all kinds of work.[3] Many people are unaware that they are getting OJT, as management refers to it, because often the education is informal. A new worker may be encouraged to hang around and try out a machine, or refer to a more experienced buddy for answers to questions. Workers call this "learning by osmosis," "gaining experience," or "working one's way up for promotion."

Since OJT depends upon old workers to train new ones, the management needs a way to assure those with more experience that they won't be knocked out of a job completely by a more talented or avid newcomer.[4] Consequently, elaborate systems of promotion develop that require minimal time experience in various slots. And the old worker knows that no matter how good a new worker is, he or she won't take home a larger pay envelope. In effect, the company has set up noncompeting groups of workers, arranged by age or experience on the job.

OJT may seem inefficient on the surface because it requires work groups to accommodate and interrupt their activity to train the newcomer. In fact, it is more productive than classroom training, because its instruction addresses the materials, machines, and situations the worker will actually face once on her own. For example, in any work involving technology, work crews discover the idiosyncrasies of a particular machine or process; they teach the newcomer how to anticipate problems with it and what repairs work best. OJT also saves unnecessary learning—information that is theoretically important but, practically speaking, of little use. Finally, through OJT, supervisors directly observe the worker in action and deduce more about her skills than a psychological test would demonstrate.

Not all jobs with OJT will result in promotional ladders and security. For example, maintenance work is thought of as a trivial job anyone can do. Employers reason that as long as people are willing to hire on for the job, it matters little whether experienced workers stay or not—they haven't that much to pass on, and they can find similar work elsewhere. Yet their rationale is actually faulty. As divorced men soon discover once they take over their own apartments, maintenance requires much specialized knowledge. Custom, not rationality, guides management here.

In such jobs as typing, employers also belittle skill. You either type well or you don't, and if you do, typing "better" does not mean a great deal at pay time. And because so many women type, new employees are readily available to replace the disgruntled ones. So administrators have little to gain by providing large incentives or promotional opportunities to clerical workers.

Once a firm is established, both employers and workers will accept some practices as the normal and best solutions to problems. Customs emerge—"That's just the way we do things here," or "That's not our style." These explanations often define everyone's agreement as to what is fair or just in the treatment of workers—equal pay for equal work, last hired–first fired, overtime to those with the most seniority, and so on. Curious idiosyncrasies bloom in some companies, such as a preference for certain colored suits on men or hairstyles on women. The "good" employee is not the one who performs skillfully, but the one who fits the company image.

It is wrong to think these definitions of fairness come only from above. Workers themselves develop their own methods of presenting themselves and performing tasks, and will sabotage newcomers who violate these practices. They can disrupt production or use union pressure to force management's formal approval of their way of working.

To the extent that workers within a job ladder are similar in background, out-of-work ideas and beliefs spill over into work-place culture. When the only persons in the sales force are Waspish men, and deals are made in men's clubs, bars, and on golf courses, then persons who normally don't participate in those settings are seen as unfit. In a society where people are raised to be fearful of those who look or act differently from one's self, these homogeneous arrangements provide workers with a sense of security and ease. However, companies can exploit worker prejudice. By selecting applicants similar in social backgrounds, bosses can be more sure that older workers will be willing to train younger ones. And by assorting blacks into one set of jobs, and whites into another, employers can stimulate cohesiveness within units, and play off workers' fears to the company's economic advantage.

Job ladders and their accompanying rewards are so beneficial that workers as well as employers strive to increase them. Employers continually modify and add to the rules and regulations for the hiring, transfer, and promoting of employees. Workers encourage their unions to fight for seniority, strict entrance requirements, control over layoffs, and other practices that build predictability to their career expectations. The result is a split within firms, where workers within well-defined job ladders have rights and privileges denied to those outside them. Advance in protected jobs comes automatically, so long as one conforms sufficiently to the model of a good worker— which may have little to do with diligence, perseverance, creativity, or productivity. When the economy slumps, protected workers are most immune from layoff or shortened work weeks.

Employers can recoup the costs of securing the loyalty of protected workers by withholding benefits from others. Additional profits accrue when all employers informally agree on which particular groups of workers will be placed in unprotected jobs, and identify the same jobs as unprotected. Thus, women and minorities are at a disadvantage because employers everywhere follow the practice of placing these workers in lower slots in the organization. If there were two large employers in a small city, and one gave minorities equal opportunity, then the other employer could no longer offer only low-paying jobs to people of special backgrounds. Given a consensus among employers on this matter, disadvantaged people are crowded into competition for poorer jobs, their fate to fight for the opportunity to work itself, not to work at fulfilling and uplifting labor.[5]

By agreeing that the same jobs will be unprotected, employers further their advantage even more. While janitorial labor does require skills, such jobs are universally denigrated. Were a major employer to reevaluate the job and pay it accordingly, other firms in that labor market would no longer be assured that their workers would remain satisfied with their low pay.

In bureaucratic work places, the separation of workers into protected and vulnerable groups has been institutionalized. In large corporations, the former may be called "exempt employees."[6] Upon joining the company, they have lengthy orientation programs in which they are given the history of the firm, taken on tours, and entertained. From the start they earn more money than nonexempt employees with many years of loyalty to the firm (though they must also spend part of this money on expensive clothing for work). Their offices are well-furnished, carpeted, and draped, with more room than their work requires. They have special dining rooms, or can eat out of the building, taking an extended lunch. When one such employee has a personal crisis, such as a divorce or alcoholism, the company may wrap itself protectively around him and provide resources to get through the difficulty.

Nonexempt employees share work space, which may be too cramped for efficient job performance. They are paid by the hour, and their time is closely watched. They eat in the company cafeteria, where their casual dress enhances the sparse surroundings. Their personal troubles are their own, a potential blemish on their work record.

Though no one in these companies moves from salesclerk to chairman of the board, promotions are a normal occurrence. The problem is that the amount of opportunity depends upon where one comes in. Organizations are not the pyramids drawn in formal charts. Were that the case, no one would bother to try for advancement because any fool can see there's only room for one at the top. So almost every job is given at least the illusion of mobility. The woman college graduate who applies to a publishing firm and is told to come in as a secretary and work herself into an editorship will at best work herself up to a larger desk and a more spacious office—as a secretary. Just as noncommissioned officers don't become colonels, file clerks don't become department managers. Jobs are walled off from one another, so the trick of succeeding without really trying is to land a job that has the most exits to other jobs with exits to still other positions. This is how people rise to their level of incompetence; they land a job that leads to better ones.

Job ladders are established through both explicit administrative decisions and informal agreements. At AT&T prior to its lawsuit, one of two paths led to the administrative ranks: being hired as a management trainee, or moving up through a crafts position. Women were not hired for either position, and thus were automatically ineligible for promotion into administration. It was not necessary for someone to say outright, "If we want to keep out the girls, all we have to do is write them out of the requirements." The promotion guidelines simply blocked female promotions whether management was aware of this or not; managerial intent is beside the point. (This is why federal equal opportunity regulations require employers to examine their promotion policies for clauses that exclude disadvantaged groups in practice, independent of conscious intent.)

Although someone may be in a slot that seems to promise mobility, the actual chances of mobility occurring will also depend upon the history of the firm and its economic situation. For example, in some manufacturing companies, sales personnel have more clout because their actions have the appearance, whether true or not, of having the primary influence on company profits, whereas in a new firm the research and development people may have more sway. Smart games players are those who can deduce these informal influences and ride with their current.[7]

Furthermore, no matter how specifically laid out in formal rules or in grapevine knowledge, job ladder practices are vulnerable to the larger culture. In school teaching, social work, and librarianship, women are the bulk of the employees, yet the administrators who have come up through the ranks are disproportionately male. These men have benefited from the general belief that males should be the leaders and are better administrators. Accordingly, if a large number of minority-group members or women suddenly find entry into a job, then chances are its pay scale and promotion ladders will change. Because women and people of color are considered inferior by society, any work they do is not to be granted the same security and opportunity as that of white men.

From this discussion of job ladders, more errors in the American Dream are clear. In protected jobs, reward comes regardless of personal effort or talent; in other jobs, chances of long-term reward and promotion are nonexistent. The workers in this latter group compete with each other; they are the women, minorities, and others of disadvantage who have more difficulty finding any job, let alone one with a long job ladder. If they hold specialized skills, such as clerical ones, then so do many others. If their work is readily transferrable, such as waiting in a restaurant, then they are likely to be in a job that does not have great rewards. If they apply themselves and work diligently, they may find themselves with some security, but little in the way of steady pay advances or increase in job responsibility.

It is because of on-the-job training, job ladders, and their related employee practices that the best predictor of lifetime income is the job one holds. Jobs cluster into families. Many are impoverished, some are moderately secure, and a few are lavishly well-to-do. Picking a first job is like being born into one of these lineages. The chances of the American Dream coming true hold only for those who pick or, more accurately, are accepted into, the best family to begin with.

THE PARASITIC ECONOMY[8]

If the moral to the previous section is "Watch the work you get," the precept for this one would be "Watch the employer who chooses you as well." For economic and historical reasons, one type of employer has reason to encourage a stable, happy work force, regardless of cost. As a result, workers are segregated not only within individual corporations, schools, and factories, they are segregated in the economy at large.

Contemporary economy in the United States is divided into two segments. One consists of relatively small enterprises, usually dominated by a single individual or family. These firms are similar to those written about by classical economists in the nineteenth century, when most goods were manufactured in small batches to meet special orders. Typically, these firms produce only a small line of related products in a highly competitive market. Their management is centralized, and its talents are concentrated at the top positions. Their major capital is human labor, not machinery. Such companies typically do not have units scattered all over the country. They might include a glove-making firm in New York City, a ring factory in Providence, a novelty manufacturer in Houston, a rubber-stamp shop in Los Angeles. Drive around any city, large or small, and you will see hundreds of such firms.

Though very different in what they produce, these firms share similar economic requirements. Being small and competitive, they must calculate on a short-term basis. They lack the liquidity to see them through difficult times. Since their major form of capital is human labor, the primary device for cutting costs is to control the labor force—by keeping wages down and benefits at a minimum, discouraging job mobility, relying upon part-time or seasonal workers, and using layoffs and firings as control valves. They are not companies that can achieve unlimited growth, because they lack the capital to invest in the technology that can move production into one more dependent upon machines than persons. Also, they do not have the secure financial position to get them a favorable interest rate at the banker's desk.

But many of these companies run satisfactorily and well in this style of operation. The managers, often owners, enjoy the challenge of complete control over the firm. If crafty and talented, they can secure substantial incomes for themselves. In many cases, the firm is tied to family connections, so that it offers the social and psychological rewards of working with kin and carrying on a bloodline tradition. In a society that seems beset with mass institutions, these firms offer rare rewards to those with entrepreneurial skills.

In some cases, such companies become exceptionally secure in spite of the market pressures. A notable example is the Maytag company. Located in Newton, Iowa, it makes primarily two products, washers and dryers. Although its competition includes such corporate giants as General Electric, Whirlpool,

American Motors, General Motors, and Ford, Maytag captures about ten percent of the market, and has developed a reputation among consumer groups for producing highly efficient and reliable machines. Part of the firm's success is that it does not follow corporation practices like marketing a new line every year or producing a wide range of models. Given its established success, Maytag can afford some of the production techniques of larger companies, and thus can support a stable labor force.

The garden-variety market firm is in very different straits. For example, the glove manufacturer is at the whim of changing fashions and the weather. The decisions of a large organization, such as the U.S. military, can force an overnight loss of a market or revamping of a design. With all this flux and lack of control over demand, the owner can seldom keep production steady throughout the year. Rather, she must often arrange production in spurts, to meet ephemeral market desires.

Clearly the worker in the glove factory is precariously employed. First, the jobs are seldom highly skilled, so experience does not count for a great deal. Thus one is easily replaceable in times of high unemployment. Second, advancement into positions of greater responsibility and reward is rare. Also, the work is not regular and predictable. (Vacations are known as layoffs.) Fourth, the employer has few incentives to meet employee demands for better work conditions or such benefits as medical insurance coverage. These firms have higher rates of quits, absenteeism, layoffs, and firings, for the simple reason that it is to the employer's advantage to have turnover in the labor force.

Economists call these establishments "peripheral firms," implying that they are not very important. While peripheral firms dominated the economy at the turn of the century, they are now subsidiary to the two other major economic actors, the government and the corporations. Some peripheral firms are subcontractors for large industries. For example, automobile dealerships or auto upholstery firms are directly dependent upon the decisions of the four auto companies in this country. Others are "loyal opposition"—companies like Maytag which have managed to develop a small part of the market, enough for their viability, though not enough to undercut the large companies. Though competitors, these loyal oppositions are dependent upon the actions of the large companies nonetheless, for example in setting prices. Finally, many peripheral firms are free agents. A recent example of this type is the company that is developed when a small group of engineers or technical experts come up with an innovation and develop their own company to market it. This last group is particularly prone to failure because the founders seldom realize that the demand for one product is often short-lived. (The clever entrepreneur must be ready to change with the market, but many free agents lack the resources or know-how to do so.)

Considering the role of peripheral firms, the name seems poorly chosen. Since their owners and managers are willing to work in a risky sector of the economy, most of the innovations in industry come from this sector, not the large companies. Probably some of the most dazzling business dealing, though invisible to most of us, occurs here. This is a part of the economy where individuals still retain autonomy in many companies, and can, by their guile or lack of it, determine an organization's health. Here is where the old-styled capitalism and free enterprise continue to thrive. For these reasons, a better name might be "market firms," a term that better reflects their competitive position.

By handling the messier jobs in the economy, market firms contribute to the security of large corporations. The market managers ply their trade in old buildings on back streets of cities, their activity hidden from public view, the only visible sign of life being a line in the yellow pages. Meanwhile, corporation officers sit in office towers that dominate the local skyline and pour their budgets into advertising that splashes through the nationwide media. Ford, General Motors, Dow Chemical, Eastman Kodak, General Electric, Sperry Rand, Kennecott Copper, Litton Industries, Gulf, Standard Oil of New Jersey, Texaco, IBM, ITT, RCA, and the other alphabetic firms were all unknown at the time of the Robber Barons, yet today have multinational entanglements.

Most of these companies, known as "center firms," began as classical capitalist endeavors. The Ford Corporation is a good example.[9] Henry Ford was a rural lad of wit and invention, who was at mid-life before he parlayed his resources into an auto-mobile manufacturing shop. The first Ford products were essentially hand-crafted by teams of highly skilled technicians. As demand grew, competition increased, and the kinks in the system straightened out, Ford sought a faster and more efficient way to produce more cars. His answer, inspired by a visit to the Chicago stockyards where he saw cattle carcasses dangling on hooks from a moving conveyor belt, was the moving assembly line. By keeping men in one place to perform the same task repeatedly, and letting the product move from station to station, Ford was able to make then unbelievable increases in production. In 1914, the company rolled 1,000 cars a day out of its doors; by 1916, the daily quota was 2,000. By changing the mode of production from unit and small batch to mass and large batch, Ford soon dominated the auto market.

His next move was to gain control over those features of the process that caused unexpected and undesirable delays, particularly in the raw materials area. Thus the company expanded to include rubber plantations in South America, forests in North America, and coal mines. It started its own steel mill. This diversification provided protection from the vicissitudes of supply availability.

In order to run a conglomerate of interrelated companies such as these, a new management system was required. Losing interest in auto production, Ford preferred to put his time in rural projects, such as the design of a cheap tractor (which would, when marketed by the company, add further to its versatility), and progressive innovations, such as starting a trade school for mechanics that paid students for their work, or developing a policy to hire ex-convicts. By the 1920s the company was run by a small committee, whose job was not to calculate short-run gains, as Ford did in his early years, but the long-term viability of the firm. Consequently, decisions were made far from the actual place of production, by people uninvolved in the direct process of manufacture.

Given these changes in structure, production, and management, the position of the worker was naturally affected. When Ford first introduced the assembly line, the skilled workers balked somewhat at the deterioration of their responsibilities and the threat that less skilled people would take their place. Ironically, Ford believed that machines eliminated human drudgery and freed people to live the good life. With the profits from increased production, he raised wages to an unheard-of $5 a day, making himself the enemy of many other companies in the country. This pay attracted a core of devoted employees, but they had to work under conditions that were less satisfying to the human spirit.

Given his engineering interests, Ford appreciated similar men of efficiency. One of his assistants developed a system for timing every move each worker made to a quarter of a second. Such calculations were at the heart of efficiency engineering. Frank and Lillian Gilbreth, parents of the cheaper dozen, were then busy injecting such labor-saving devices into industry. The labor was not what was saved—it was the company that saved in the gains made by the method, through the profits earned with each increase in productivity. (Mr. Gilbreth aptly illustrated the effects of the technique on labor when he died of a heart attack at a relatively young age.)

As years passed, the Ford management imposed other methods of control upon workers. It speeded up the assembly line without concern for the maximal efficiency of work. It forbade talking on the job and introduced the types of petty and odious regulations one recalls from the school days of childhood. It used the ex-convicts as spies. It determinedly snuffed out any spark of unionism.

The Ford company's success rested more with management's wisdom in responding to competition than with its handling of employees. For example, during the twenties, when General Motors made large advances by following Alfred Sloan's directive of producing new models each year, Ford responded by building the largest factory in the world. To decrease its costs, it purchased the Johnson Gauge Company, which provided the technology to combine mass production with the fine precision Ford himself valued.

Ford employees, like those of other auto manufacturers, were required to bend to each addition of technology. Jobs grew more segmented and less specialized. The man whose father had built an entire car was now lucky if he turned more than a few bolts on a chassis. When the workers protested, the companies used their economic influence to persuade political authorities to bring in police and National Guard to break up demonstrations, even at the cost of lives. They would rather sanction murder than allow workers a voice in determining the conditions of labor. The workers and their spouses fought back undeterred, and eventually won.[10]

In 1941, Ford workers received their first labor union contracts, marking the final stage in the company's development as a mature center firm, the securing of a stable work force. Because a company of this scope and differentiation can control its operations to ensure a continual cash flow, it can cover the costs of employee demands, indeed seek to meet them so as to minimize labor unrest. Thus larger center firms in manufacturing have strong unions attached to them, and the nonunion workers, usually white-collar, technical and managerial people, enjoy higher wages than they would in market firms. Wages are proportionately not as large a component of costs to center firms, so labor is not manipulated in the same way as in the periphery. Rather, management develops a paternalistic attitude toward its workers; in some large companies today, employees can obtain free psychological counseling, alcohol rehabilitation, tuition and time off for education, and the use of health club facilities on company property. Seldom are large numbers of center firm workers laid off or fired. Indeed, the very threat of such, as sometimes happens in the steel or auto industries, is taken as a serious sign of potential recession by the government, which takes steps to minimize such occurrences.

THE HANDICAPPED SOCIETY

Segregated job arrangements explain why education doesn't pay off for women and minority workers. They don't get placed in the same jobs as equally educated white men, and they never have the same career opportunities. In effect, the system works opposite to its claims. The people who start out life with a break get even more as they progress through adulthood. It's as though the best golfers were given the better handicaps.

Even when disadvantaged workers manage to find more privileged jobs, they are most likely to land up in a market firm. Consequently, when women break into crafts work, they are less likely to be hired by large, solvent contractors, so they earn less and work less than men with the same training and experience.

White men are similarly affected by segregated job structures. A white male working in a market firm earns $4,100 less a year than his counterpart in a center firm. A bad job or a job in a competitive firm pays white males little more than women or minorities. This is why the key to economic inequality rests ultimately with disadvantaged jobs, not disadvantaged workers.[11]

Correlatively, those minority members and women who make it to better jobs or work in the central firms enjoy more job security or higher pay than their kin—though not as much as white men. A good job, or any job in a good company, rewards white men more than others. For this reason, personal characteristics of workers cannot be eliminated altogether from consideration of policies to increase economic equality.

The segregated job market provokes social as well as economic forces to perpetuate inequality. Privileged workers—those with better jobs or with jobs in the central economy—are oblivious to the work life of others. They fail to understand the benumbing, insecure, poorly-paid lot that other hard-working Americans endure daily. Since they enjoy some mobility, however illusory, and a comfortable, if not affluent life style, they attribute their success to their own efforts, and damn those who fail. As people who come from privileged positions in society, policy makers and social scientists are just as likely to buy this self-serving myth and overlook the ocean of data that drowns its meaning in disproof.

Center firms further encourage this sense of superiority by attacking the social welfare system. They have sold workers that government welfare is sinful; corporate welfare is not. "You deserve these social benefits because you are good workers for us," they say, "not because you are human beings in a society that espouses freedom from want." At the same time they are careful to allow sufficient welfare to meet, however, meagerly, the needs of those in disadvantaged jobs. Thus the system hobbles forward, with the center firms gaining the major economic benefit. The government is an emergency aid for unfortunate workers, and the corporation binds worker loyalty by showing its largesse to its advantaged workers. If there were genuine welfare in this country, employers would have a hard time filling their ranks, for the quality of work has deteriorated so much in America that it is only through corporate welfare and the encouragement of false superiority that its workers remain.[12]

Those in advantaged jobs rest securely with full stomachs at the direct expense of workers kept out of the privileged job market. The dry-cleaning employee works at low wages, and may find himself laid off from time to time as a result of the exigencies of fashion, yet even when employed he cannot afford dry cleaning himself. An enormous invisible servant class is developing: maids, cooks, and butlers have been supplanted by personal service specialties. Those who provide our most basic needs—the food gatherers and clothing makers—are among the least rewarded. Unlike several centuries ago, they do not even have respect from others for doing a job well, however low its station. They may take pride in their work, but when others do not care, the temptation to merely get the job done desanctifies their labor. They are completely in the bind described by Albert Camus in *The Stranger:* "Without work all life goes rotten. But when work is soulless, life stifles and dies."

Chapter 9

Federal Hypocrisy

Equal Employment opportunity is the law. It is mandated by Federal, State, and local legislation, Presidential Executive Orders and definitive court decisions.
Government affirmative action guidebook
for employers

It bespeaks great weakness if you try to straighten out someone else's closet when your own is not in order.
Abelardo Perez,
Mexican American Legal Defense
and Educational Fund

The nation's largest civilian employer is the federal government, and its labor practices traditionally set the tone for those of state and local governments. At first look, one would expect women and minorities to do well in government service. Most positions are in the competitive civil service, a system that expressly prohibits discrimination toward women and blacks. Government offices are located in downtown metropolitan areas, making them physically accessible to minority workers residing in cities. And in recent years, the growing political power of women and minorities has put pressure on federal and local governments to increase their hiring and promotions.[1]

Nonetheless, the discriminatory patterns found in other firms pervade government. Although minorities have the same chance to get a federal job (though not a good one) as other kinds of work, women have a more difficult time obtaining employment.[2] One reason here may be the veterans' preference, which places veterans ahead of better scoring competitors on employment lists. Consequently, a woman who performs at the top of an examination and interview may not be hired until veterans with acceptable—though lower—grades are hired first. This preference follows workers through a lifetime, thus providing an advantage at every stage in their government career.

Here a well-meaning policy unintentionally discriminates against one large class of workers, women, simply because few veterans are women.

More frequently women are disadvantaged in government for the same reason they are in private firms—job segregation. In civil service, jobs are graded into eighteen rankings; the lower the rank, the lower the presumed skill and pay. The average grade for a government worker in 1977 was 8.22. For women it was 5.93, and for blacks, 6.32.[3] When women and minorities have been promoted to higher ranks, it has usually been to those functions dealing with equal employment or social services. (Executive appointments reflect this bias as well. Consequently, we've seen a black woman appointed to be head of the Department of Housing and Urban Development, but would be most surprised to see one assigned to Agriculture or Defense.) When women or members of minority groups work in embassies overseas, they issue visas and rescue American tourists in trouble; they do not act as political or economic attachés.

The experiences of workers at one agency—Health, Education, and Welfare—suggest the extent of the problem. In the early seventies, though women comprised 63 percent of all HEW employees, nine out of ten were in the dead-end jobs below the GS-9 mark. Even highly educated women in the agency failed to receive parity with men; women with Ph.D.'s and M.D.'s were not assigned as administrators of research projects. Similarly, nearly half of those in the very bottom jobs (GS-4 and below) were black women.

Angered by the HEW conditions, a group of workers took their case to *Science,* one of the country's most prestigious journals in that field.[4] Their stories were similar to those told by hospital, college, factory, and store employees. One woman with a doctorate in science was informed she could not become permanent chief of the unit she had been overseeing because "they need an M.D., but the man who replaced me is not an M.D. Also, he has had less than one year's experience at NIH [National Institutes of Health] and is ten to fifteen years younger than I am." When one field office designated a woman as acting supervisory inspector, every man under her called in sick. One researcher told an eminent woman scientist that he never discriminated against women in his lab because "you get more talent for the buck. Women are usually willing to come in at lower grade levels than men." When she looked at his lab, she noted indeed a proliferation of well-educated women hired as low-level lab technicians. Eliot Richardson, then head of HEW, made a remark (which he later publicly regretted) that it was his impression women did not want responsibility, as he hardly ever saw them on commuter flights between New York and Washington.

Not all women in HEW approved of the public disclosure but remained silent, perhaps in fear for their jobs. But as physician Estelle Ramey explained, "If you see yourself as a researcher under a great male scientist and he treats you well, then you don't think you're discriminated against; but if you think you should have the same options as men with similar talents and experience, then you realize you are. Equality in'job situations will come when female mediocrity moves along at the same rate as male mediocrity—not when a female Einstein makes it."

These examples are all the more telling when one considers that HEW is one of the most equalitarian agencies in the federal government in terms of rank and income parity to women and minorities![5] Only two agencies have better records—the Equal Employment Opportunity Commission and the State Department.

The most disadvantageous agencies for workers other than white males are those dealing with defense, agriculture, transportation, and space—all fields identified with masculine virtues. Even the Justice Department, which plays a role in prosecuting discrimination cases, fares badly. The very worst agency overall is NASA, which made front-page headlines and color photographs in the news magazines in 1978 with its pictures of the first female and black astronaut trainees. These press releases were curiously self-congratulatory in tone, as though the agency thought it deserved a medal for a superficial sign of awareness of its previous errors.

Though the statistics are disappointing, on an overall basis women and minority-group members who break into government do bring home more pay than their neighbors working with other bosses in their communities. In 1977, half of all women in full-time federal jobs earned $11,500, compared to their counterparts' $8,200 in the private sector. Still, their lifetime career opportunities are limited, their chances for administrative positions almost zero. Consequently, charges of discrimination against agencies are common; in 1977 alone, the number of race- and sex-bias claims by federal employees numbered 47,500. The majority of cases accused those very agencies with the most unbending records on civil rights, such as the military bureaucracies. When attempts at reconciliation failed, 8,000 of these cases moved on to the EEOC, which faced the onerous task of handslapping another agency of government. (This outcome is rare, however, because Congress has designed a convoluted and time-delaying procedure for grievances by federal workers, which serves well to let complaints die before any effective cure is applied.)

These employees are luckier than those of a decade ago. When Congress drafted the Civil Rights Act of 1964, it conveniently omitted federal agencies from its jurisdiction. Although the following year Lyndon Johnson signed an executive order requiring equal opportunity in the government, he included no procedures for redress of employee grievances. It was not until 1972 that Congress brought federal workers under the umbrella of affirmative action and allowed them to press suit against an agency if disputes could not be resolved. Thus, for eight years the government was ordering private employers to comply with regulations that did not apply to itself. With the regulator free to discriminate, employers could hardly be expected to take the regulations seriously.

These facts should not be surprising. We all know that no women have ever been elected president or named Supreme Court justices, and there are few woman generals, cabinet members, or senators. Nor have we had many dark-skinned faces in these offices. If the chiefs all look alike, we can hardly expect less of the troop commanders. How much can we expect of a government that until two decades ago maintained segregated employee lunchrooms, separate seniority and promotion lines by race, and the explicit exclusion of women from all but the most perfunctory jobs? What gains can be expected in a country, where, when I was growing up, a white male could hope to be president—provided he wasn't Catholic or Jewish?

If the electoral and appointive processes have failed to replace a representative selection of Americans in high offices, so too have the legislative and administrative branches neglected to give employees equal opportunity. A House committee in 1977 charged that congressional staff members worked in what was effectively the last plantation system in the country. When black and white employees were matched for skill and training, the black employee in every case was earning less than the comparable white. In jobs paying more than $35,000 yearly, men outnumbered women 15 to 1. The Elizabeth Ray scandal, which gave public proof to the gossip that some congressmen had hired women for other than strictly professional purposes, must be matched by the larger scandal that the majority of congressmen overwork and underreward their female or minority aides and assistants. Hirings in legislative offices are immune from the usual equal opportunity regulations, and to date the congress seems content to enjoy their patriarchal privileges. (As of 1979, only one of every four House members had signed a pledge to practice fair employment).[6]

PLANNED INEPTITUDE

Federal recalcitrance to practice equal employment in its own house repeats itself in legislation and agency procedures. It is as though plantation owners were handed control of freeing the slaves. Elected officials and agency heads have covered over their unconcern or inability to take action with sweet talking.

Shoddy actions and motives defame the very history of Title VII of the Civil Rights Act of 1964. Most notable was Representative Howard Smith's introduction of the word "sex" into the bill as a joke; his hope was to provoke so much dissension and debate over the granting of equal employment to women that the entire act would collapse in defeat. Wily last-minute lobbying by feminists and civil rights leaders, as well as an unexpected coalition of conservative and liberal female legislators, cut off that assault. Nevertheless, Congress waited eight more years to give the EEOC the power to implement law suits.[7]

Loopholes limit the intent of this bill and other regulations that followed it.[8] Title VII is unusually sweeping on the surface; basically it forbids discrimination in advertising, hiring, upgrading, salaries, fringe benefits, training, and other conditions of employment. Its coverage includes private employers, governments, employment agencies, and labor unions. However, it exempts firms with less than 15 employees. Consequently, the small businessperson can say, as one architect I know did to a woman in his firm, "When I add my fifteenth coworker, I'll pay you the same as I pay men in your job." This exclusion particularly affects workers in small communities, or those who do not have commuting mobility to take a job with a larger firm outside their neighborhood. The EEOC is to investigate, resolve, and, if necessary, litigate complaints; it may also encourage employers to develop voluntary compliance programs. In other words, employers can take their chances that no claims will be pressed.

The other major set of regulations (Executive Orders 11246 and 11375) concerns firms doing federal contracts of $10,000 or more, as well as banks handling federal savings bonds and monies. The demands of Title VII apply with one addition: employers are to demonstrate that they are taking affirmative action to remedy the effects of past discrimination. The Office of Federal Contract Compliance can do onsite reviews as well as investigate complaints. If the employer fails to meet agency standards, it can be debarred from receiving future contracts. Though strongly worded, this order has weaknesses. While implicated in the contracts, labor unions are not directly subject to the orders. Also, construction contractors have not been required to include goals for women employees in their plans. Finally, the implementation allows small contractors to keep one or two minority employees as "floaters" or bodies, to make the statistics look good. (Women clerks have been listed in payrolls as construction workers.)

Complicating the regulatory picture further, yet other acts grant special rights and specify a particular agency to oversee their guarantee. The Equal Pay Act of 1973 is regulated by the

Wage and Hours Division of the Department of Labor. Four separate sets of regulations govern the rights of federal employees, and come under the control of the U.S. Civil Service Commission. Another act covers workers in state cooperative extension services, and is managed by the Department of Agriculture. And it is curious in the light of our knowledge of union practices that Congress passed an act, obviously ignored, forbidding discrimination in all state-registered apprenticeship programs back in 1937!

The problems with this division of responsibility are obvious. First is the simple fact that workers don't know their legal rights and how to ensure them. While the federal government makes sure employers receive copies of regulations and guidelines, they do not so inform the public. (Although I've long considered myself an expert on discrimination policies, even I discovered new material while going through obscure publications from the U.S. Commission on Civil Rights.) Among the best book buys available, government documents are not disseminated in the manner one would expect of a democracy. Nor does the media take seriously its responsibility to inform the public of its rights and options as changes in law and administration occur daily in legislatures and agencies around the country. China, with its mural walls of important announcements, does a better job of reaching its people.

Further hampering good public contact, the EEOC operates out of only seven regional offices, making it physically inaccessible to most workers. Nor does it provide toll-free phone service to facilitate communication.

Also, jurisdictional disputes may arise in a specific case. The varieties of discrimination seldom occur solitarily; a case of unequal pay will likely be one of unequal promotion as well. Does the EEOC or the Wage and Hour Division of the Department of Labor take charge? Attempts to resolve one common jurisdictional dispute, that between state and federal agencies, introduce further delay and inefficiency. When the EEOC receives a complaint, it refers the matter to local agencies for sixty days. Thus papers pass through the mails, from file cabinet to out box, with all the attendant possibilities for loss, inattention, or misdirection.

Furthermore, the proliferation of agencies complicates employers' activities as well. Each agency has its own accounting demands and required forms as evidence that the regulations are being followed. Consequently, employers of large firms have added affirmative action offices for the purposes of implementing the regulations, collecting relevant statistics, and filing appropriate forms. Corporations can add this new unit with little difficulty—they regularly incorporate new functions into their bureaucracies and have the capital to allow such expansion. But for hospitals, schools, and small companies in the market economy, the staff and resources committed to meeting government accounting regulations cut into the budget for essential services. Consequently, those firms that play a significant role in the work lives of women and minorities are the most disadvantaged by current federal requirements, which pressure tight budgets.

These complications matter only if the federal enforcement is a serious one to begin with. As will be shown in more detail in the next section, the record indicates otherwise. Astute politicians know that one way to mollify a noisy interest group is to pass its bill and then grant little funding for its implementation. Lack of money and staffing has persistently tied the hands of the various equal opportunity agencies since their inception. Though federal expenditures for civil rights enforcement have increased since the destructive lows of the Nixon reign, the budgets do not yet allow for a sufficient processing of claims. In fact, civil-rights allocations account for only five-tenths of one percent of all federal money allocated to social needs. Yet no more easily could Congress alleviate problems of poverty, ill-health, and crime than by vigorous enforcement of equal work and equal pay laws.[9]

Part of the problem is political. No administration to date has taken a strong stance on equal employment, rhetoric to the contrary. Even Lyndon Johnson, under whose administration the 1964 Civil Rights Act was passed, did not pass on the clout the agencies needed. As a result programs are administered by oldtime civil service bureaucrats who themselves have come up the ranks through the benefits of discrimination, and thus cannot be expected to push private employers and contractors to atone for their past errors.

This interference was evident in one of the most important early civil rights lawsuits, that involving the claims of blacks against the Newport News Shipyard, a defense contractor.[10] This was the first opportunity for Johnson to display his muscle over the elimination of racial inequality on the job. In obtaining the company's concession to the promotion of 3,000 black employees who had repeatedly been passed over, and to the listing of 100 black workers on the foremen's list for the first time, the administration worked out a forceful conciliation model for future cases. But it let other forces disrupt the chances for similar advancements.

At that time the Department of Defense was in charge of monitoring its own contracts, and the military generals balked at pursuing any more cases. Instead, they diluted the power of equal opportunity activities by scattering their functions throughout the Pentagon's behemoth form. Then they dispensed with their most effective and tough-minded enforcement officer. And in a brilliant administrative move, they ruled that if a company could show that compliance with equal opportunity would hamper production, the production needs would take priority. Thus, any defense contractor need only certify that operations would be interrupted or less efficient as a result of affirmative action changes—a relatively simple matter for administrators talented with the manipulation of words and statistics.

The recalcitrance of the Defense Department was not trivial to federal enforcement. It handled over 75 percent of federal contracts, and was responsible for the activities of 30,000 establishments. Yet it had so few staff committed to compliance review that only about half of the contractors in any one year underwent perfunctory examination, so it is possible that some employers were never checked during the life of a contract.

The federal record on contract compliance further reflects bureaucratic and political snafus. Over a nine-year period, only twenty-one of the thousands of federal contractors were actually debarred from further service; just three of these were companies of notable size or monopoly power: American Sanitary, Ingersoll Mining, and Uniroyal.[11] Each year less than one percent of contractors have been asked to "show cause" as to why they should not be debarred. Given the pervasive discrimination at work places in our country, this enforcement is equivalent to cleaning a large wound by placing a drop of antiseptic solution here and there, now and then. The infection remains virulent.

Fortunately, one sign of improvement occurred in 1978.[12] Then, as part of its bureaucratic simplification program, the Carter administration brought federal contract compliance activities, previously scattered among twelve agencies, under the Office of Federal Contract Compliance Programs, which had served merely as an overseer to that point. Personnel and budgetary allotments were transferred as well as functions. The Office then established seventy-one local outlets for complaint processing, developed a computerized information system, provided the first comprehensive compliance manual for employers, and added women to the construction contractor timetables. Their enforcement record doubled that of previous years, but whether this move is more than an initial enthusiasm remains to be seen. (To double a very poor record still leaves one in a bad place overall.)

Federal inaction pervades other agencies. A notable case is the Treasury Department, which is responsible for civil rights compliance in banking and finance.[13] The increased employment of disadvantaged people in these firms is necessary, not just for individual workers and their families, but also to break down entrenched prejudice in lending circles that keeps investment money out of the hands of women and minorities. Yet the record on equal employment in these firms is among the worst.

When the Women's Equality Action League in 1972 filed a class action suit with the Treasury Department against twenty-seven Dallas banks for sex discrimination, the agency sent eight men to investigate. In a bald-faced ploy of compliance, one apparently acceptable to the Treasury, several of the banks promoted women to their boards the day before the reviewers arrived. The department later refused to report its findings to W.E.A.L. In discussing the case, a compliance officer (a woman) told the Council on Economic Priorities, "Oh, those ladies. They do upset me."

In another case, the day after the EEOC filed suit against the Bank of America—a suit which was later to settle out of court, in favor of minority and women employees—the head of the Treasury Department's compliance section held a news conference to praise the bank's affirmative-action program. The bank had no such program at that time.

Although independent researchers have found extensive and unmistakable bias at banking institutions, Treasury has never denied funds to any major bank for noncompliance. No data has been made available to the public concerning which banks have been reviewed. When the Council on Economic Priorities requested such information, the Department responded that it didn't keep any records on banks that fail to comply because "there just aren't that many."

AFFIRMATIVE INACTION

In view of all these machinations and resistances to equal opportunity in the government itself, it would seem that compliance programs are essentially nasty but manageable problems for employers to get around. Studies that examine more directly the relationship between government intervention and equal opportunity verify this impression, yet add some unexpected twists. Typically, the investigators look at companies' employee policies and opportunities before and after the introduction of federal compliance activity. Thus two economists examining 3,700 firms in the Chicago-Gary area discovered a very slight improvement in the hiring of black males for firms that undertook government contracts.[14] However, the hiring rate of women, both black and white, dropped off. Also, the contract firms placed more white men in white collar jobs *after* contract compliance. Another review of almost 75,000 firms around the country uncovered a similar trend: black and white males benefited, while women and other minorities lost.[15]

These studies were done when the federal contracts aimed at improving the situation of racial minorities, before sex was included in the thrust. Consequently, it may no longer be the case that men gain at women's expense under affirmative action. Still, if the emphasis was on racial gain, one must wonder why the black women failed to improve their position in contract firms, and why other racial minorities lagged or even fell behind in equal opportunity while black men advanced. The information available cannot answer these questions, because the OFCC simply hasn't maintained the data banks that could serve investigators in a better assessment of programs. Indeed, it isn't even possible to identify what types of contractors are more likely to be obstinate or evasive.

Why then did white males fare better under contract compliance rules than without them? One answer is that the addition of regulations means that firms must create departments to implement affirmative action plans. In other words, the regulations create more managerial positions for white men to fill, allowing black men to move up into some technical slots. A more cynical, perhaps more reasonable interpretation, is that employers take such care not to injure white men's chances that they give them even more advantages than previous to contract compliance.

Overall, the economists surveying federal contract compliance practices find their impact slight. One analyst has concluded that even under the best of conditions *"a comprehensive* contract compliance program that succeeded in equalizing opportunities for minorities might directly eliminate about 30 to 40 percent of the hourly wage rate differential" between whites and others. But as he points out, the current procedures scarcely provide an efficient and comprehensive program.[16]

The other major compliance arm of equal employment regulation is by way of arbitration and litigation, with the EEOC as the intermediary agency between workers and bosses. During the seventies, the numbers of cases pressed by workers multiplied fivefold. Although a court trial is the last stage in a labyrinthine path toward solution of a grievance, over 5,000 cases made the courtroom in 1976 alone.[17] An analysis of arbitration and court solutions highlights important weaknesses in the EEOC approach. Although professionals comprise only about 12 percent of all workers in the country, they initiated over half of the suits. Most obvious, a court case is an expensive and time-consuming process, which most workers in our society cannot afford. It is also a procedure requiring tremendous personal confidence and strength under pressure, qualities discouraged among most jobholders, who are trained to see the boss as superior, correct, and invincible. Second, black males composed almost half of the grievants, or the bulk of the racial discrimination cases. Yet statistics repeatedly demonstrate that it is the minority women who incur the most disadvantage in hiring, pay, and promotion. Something in the procedures does not reach these workers.

When all the months of collecting information, dealing with lawyers, and testifying in court is over, about six in ten workers win their cases and are awarded recompense. If the case has been a class action suit, which is occurring with more frequency than was the case in the early years of civil rights, the effects of winning reach many workers—any persons who may have been affected by the proceedings. For example, when Brown University settled out of court on a charge of sex discrimination, any woman who had applied to Brown for a job over a specific time period, or who was denied promotion then, could enter a claim for damages.

The press broadcasts the results of such cases regularly enough to lead the public to think the courtroom process is an efficient and effective one. This conclusion is erroneous. A typical job litigation is fraught with denial, delay, deadlock, and detente. As of late 1979, a 1971 suit against a major San Francisco department store had not gotten into the courtrooms, a 1972 suit against United Airlines had almost gone to trial four times, still unsuccessfully, and a 1973 suit against Union Oil was still alive although the original plaintiff had died. The records show that corporations fight sex discrimination claims more aggressively than other allegations: since women workers outnumber all other disadvantaged groups combined, the costs of granting women equity are much higher.[18]

In addition to implying that lawsuits are matter-of-fact affairs, the media fails to follow up on the consequences of court cases. Consent decrees ordering firms to stop unfair practices and provide compensatory relief for past wrongs are court orders. Yet just as husbands evade child care support, employers and unions ignore compliance commitments. For example, five years after a decree setting timetables for minority hiring in Northern California construction, a judge found "a damning case of severe underrepresentation, indeed almost total exclusion, of minorities." Five years after Blue Shield of California entered a settlement to pay compensation to Filipino workers, not one claim had been processed. In another case, decided in 1976, California canneries were to create a $5 million fund to compensate women and minority workers previously excluded from permanent jobs. Four years later not one had been paid. The blame for this inaction must be laid not only with the employers and unions, but with the courts for their failure to press for accountability after judgment, and with the EEOC, which manages through its snafus and red tape to disrupt rather than facilitate the implementation of cases.

Any court case or arbitration that results in a rightful judgment, whether for the worker or the firm, is a sign of success in the system. There is no way of gauging whether a sixty-percent employee win rate reflects a fair resolution without knowing the facts of each case. That is for the omniscient to judge. Regardless of these successes, large numbers of disadvantaged workers, whether blue-collar and service employees, clerical staff, minority women, or those with disabilities, are not finding redress through these procedures. Because current federal practices operate unequally, they only contribute further to the perpetuation of economic injustice.

Chapter 10

Balms and Nostrums

As long as egalitarians assume that public policy cannot contribute to economic equality directly, but must proceed by ingenious manipulation of marginal institutions like the schools, progress will remain glacial.
Christopher Jencks, Inequality

In the sixties, education was the social panacea. Facing the awful facts of its discrimination toward minorities, the nation poured millions of dollars into schools to ensure a fairer distribution of resources so that the poor would stay in classrooms. Whether this largesse was the cause or not, students who five years earlier would have dropped out now earned diplomas. Women entered college in large numbers as well, in response both to a growing labor market and to feminist encouragement that they seek their own careers. As a result we have a more highly skilled work force, yet the inequalities remain.

What happened? Why didn't degrees open doors for the disadvantaged? In terms of the way work is structured in our society, a black is still a black, diploma or not. All the diploma did was add a new qualification to a "black job." The laborer who would have been hired without a high-school certificate in the fifties was required to hold one in the sixties. Women who wanted to become secretaries found that firms which had hired their older sisters with high-school diplomas now wanted junior-college certificates as well. The jobs didn't change in content—employers simply shifted their requirements to take into account the changes in the educational level of workers.[1]

Increased education did not improve the maldistribution of economic resources as the liberals had hoped. First, those mi-

norities who earned diplomas put those without in even more
difficult straits. Young men who quit school found they could
not get the jobs their older dropout brothers had once landed.
Survival for these youth became a swirl of drug dealing, rob-
bery, pimping, and other scams. By the time they reached
adulthood they were virtually unemployable, and faced lives of
inner turmoil behind the flashy uniform prescribed for neighborhood exploiters.

While large proportions of educated women and minorities
scoured the want ads, fewer white males filled the work force.
Since these men enjoyed jobs with substantial retirement benefits, they left full-time work at a younger age than others. This
shorter tenure opened spaces for others of their background to
move up into. As preferred workers, the smaller numbers of
white men have only made their kind more valued by employers.

Another way increased education has heightened inequality
is in terms of the quality of work life of disadvantaged and
privileged workers. In recent decades, work activities on an
overall basis have become increasingly routinized, fragmented,
and tied to the needs of machines. This proletarianization, as
some call it, has affected jobs throughout the spectrum, from
upper management to janitorial work. A simple example is the
change in the use of secretaries, who have traditionally performed many tasks for a boss or two; companies now set up
separate pools of people who type, take dictation, duplicate,
and file information. As a result, workers feel less pride in their
accomplishments, sense less meaning in their jobs, and enjoy
fewer social satisfactions than their parents did. They are too
smart for society.

Although overqualification has affected all workers, it has hit
the disadvantaged ones much harder. This has happened in
two ways. First, their traditional jobs are becoming more simplified and broken up than the jobs privileged white males
hold. Second, when they get nontraditional jobs, they are required to have more education and experience than white
males in similar positions. So again, increased education has
had the unintended effect of worsening the economic disadvantage of workers.

The problems of proletarianized work and overqualification explain the weaknesses in another proposal, namely, to give disadvantaged groups better career counseling. But how can one counsel workers who are not going to be employed in the first place? This is not a trivial problem. For example, many colleges now are courting older women to return to school and fill up spaces left by a falling birthrate. When schools are in small, localized economies, as is the school where I have taught for many years, the number of jobs for highly skilled workers are few. And because small city employers tend to be more traditional, they are less likely than firms in large cities with heterogeneous populations to change their hiring preferences. Unless the schools pressure employers to reconsider their personnel practices, they proffer false hopes to these returning students.

For younger students, there remains the problem that guidance counseling itself is not adequately prepared to provide real instruction about work opportunities. The overriding influence in the field has been the testing of the individual to point out what choices would be best for him or her. IQ tests, Kuder preference forms, and Holland interest scales separate youngsters and assort them into bins marked Brains, Brawn, Art, Sweet Young Thing, and so forth. Smart students, wealthy students, children of socially eminent or powerful parents, find themselves directed toward the high-prestige occupations, even though readily available job forecasts indicate that fields like law are headed for a glut. The country is chronically short of nurses, a job requiring much personal responsibility and adeptness, yet better students are not directed to fill that need because it bears the image of a doctor's helpmate.

And what good is counseling for students who made the mistake of being born into the wrong family? What can one say to the youngster who is going to spend her life in and out of canning factories, or his years blistering in the heat of a smelter? All one can do is let them know that they deserve the fate, and schools do that well. "General diploma" tracks are, as the youngsters know, "dummy classes." In eroding the youngster's self-esteem, the schools produce ideal workers for the peripheral jobs in the economy. These men and women go off to the factories daily with a silent sense of shame that they cannot do better. They take their penance willingly for being inadequate.

Were teachers and counselors to tell the truth about work opportunities in America, they would find themselves in an impossible job. Their ignorance is borne of their own privilege, and that they do not question the system is proof of its effectiveness in suppressing attitudes that would make for troublesome workers. Changes in counseling and schooling matter, but the transformations must be in light of the realities of work, not the mythologies.

Another recommended policy is to revamp the testing requirements for jobs so that hiring examinations are better predictors of performance. Presumably, then, a person with a special skill or interest in an activity, such as hand and finger dexterity, will be identified and hired regardless of race, creed, religion, sex, age, or disability. This is the meritocratic ideal, the world where skills match work requirements.

Certainly this procedure would be better than past ones, where laborers were given analytical reasoning examinations that had nothing to do with their physical abilities and better served to eliminate minorities from the work crews than identify capable workers. Currently, federal regulations require that any test used be validated or proven effective as a predictor of job behavior. Consequently, many once-popular personnel devices have fallen into the dust bins.[2]

Yet should we replace outmoded devices with new ones? The beneficiaries of a testing program would be psychologists and test makers, not workers. If tests were so good to begin with, then Allen Bakke would have made it into medical school solely on the basis of his excellent scores. But the testing profession has a very bad track record. It does a better job of designing rationales for keeping some groups of people from opportunities than for identifying talented people throughout the society.

Furthermore, the testing view presumes that work tasks can be analyzed and simplified to the point where a battery of items would ensure the selection of the best people. Yet anyone who has ever been an employer knows that the most suitable people on paper can be duds because of idiosyncrasies in the work place. The best predictor of how good a worker will be is his or her performance the first month on the job. To feed and encourage the testing industry at this point seems a poor use of resources, one serving more the interests of psychometricians and test producers than the interests of workers (or employers).

"Equal pay for equal work" is another popular slogan. According to this view, jobs privileged men hold should be compared with those held by other workers to see whether the former get paid more for the same job, or whether a different job title disguises the fact that both are doing the same labor at unequal wages. If implemented, this practice would touch very few workers, for the simple reason that each subordinate group is herded into its own labor market. When a third of all women and scarcely any men are secretaries, it matters little that the wages between the two are set equal. When over half the men in this country work in all-male jobs, then there simply are no women in comparable positions to raise up to the same pay level.

It may even be possible that some of the increase in job segregation of recent years is an employer reaction to equal-pay requirements. To avoid equal pay, all management need do is make sure workers are not put in the same jobs.

The preferable alternative slogans would be "Fair job assessment" and "Equal work for all," both of which will be explored in detail in the next chapter. These policies have the benefit of placing the onus for change upon the gatekeepers and employers, yet suffer for their presumption that the competitive, rigid work structure of our society is acceptable as a basis for expressing the virtues of labor. What good is "fair job assessment," when the bulk of work is meagerly rewarded, the difference between the earnings of the poorest and the best job a multiple of fifty? What use is "equal work for all" when the shifting means a few varied faces and bodies in the board rooms, and tougher competition for those white men who thus far have expected the privilege as a right? Such policies may be necessary as wedges of change, but it would take a massive implementation to burst apart the tough fibers of hierarchy.

A common informal tactic being pressed upon disadvantaged people is that they develop their personal presentation
and competitive techniques. For example, they can learn to
dress better. If that doesn't work, then maybe they need to develop some assertiveness techniques and speak in ways that
put themselves in best form. If that isn't useful, then perhaps
they are too ignorant of their marketable skills and should do a
trait-and-functions analysis of their life experiences to establish a clearer selling point for the employer. If that isn't successful, then it may be because they are lazy or inept job seekers who need only learn the new methods of job hunting
("Network," "Keep file cards," "Make five phone calls a day").
Or perhaps they are being unrealistic about the job market,
and should take minor functionary positions and prove to the
boss what great employees they are. Still not good? Perhaps it's
the resumé or interview responses.

The new career-development model only furthers the concept of the worker as a commodity or piece of capital for rent.
The spate of improvement books and life-planning counselors
testify to the demand by workers for a better lot in life. In
placing the onus of change upon the worker, these methods
only exacerbate the situation. First, to the extent that more
people become aware of these techniques, the competition
heightens. As with education, the emphasis upon personal development only inflates the value of the privileged workers,
and leaves those disadvantaged ones who are unaware of the
new game rules even more unacceptable as employees. When
women employees in increasing numbers dress up to work,
take pains to present themselves as efficient and effective workers, the employers simply gain a better quality work force at no
cost to themselves. And those women in the office who are all
pursuing the same tactics merely set a new, more demanding
standard for the others to follow.

One reason the career-development approach appears so
sensible is that failure is hard to prove. The people who study
these techniques are likely to be inquisitive, go-getter types
who would find a job no matter what. Contrary to Richard
Bolles' claim, the majority of people with disabilities—persons
with talents for all types of jobs in our society—cannot get em-

ployment no matter how diligently they develop themselves, learn to present themselves in self-effacing ways, and sell themselves with aplomb. These systems are like chain letters—the first few people make a little money because they get into the action before everyone else rides the wave.

Self-development approaches also encourage a dehumanizing view of personality, one in which only strength—as defined by employer values—is to be retained in one's self-concept. We are to suppress and eliminate those parts of ourselves that don't fit the narrow administrative definition. We are constantly like athletes in training, denying some parts of ourselves and overdeveloping others for the narrow goal of the race. We may become Olympic runners, but in the process we will lose breadth in self-expression and human sensitivity. In sum, the career-development approach, while speaking from often explicitly humane and well-intended goals, proffers solutions that only complicate the problem it purports to solve.

Many jobs in our society do not need active, assertive, competitive people. Indeed, these are exactly the types of people we don't need in libraries, research laboratories, child-care centers, old-age homes, government offices, and probably much of the business world. Effective personnel managers, those with an intuition about placing people in jobs in which both the company and the person can grow, have always known that the shy person, the very self-willed, the one oblivious to dress, and the perfectionist are not strange or inappropriate personalities, but indeed may be the preferred choice for certain kinds of jobs.

The effects of self-development expectations are obvious in business magazines and working-women's magazines. The hair, dress, and body language of male executives and women managers are monotonously similar. They are never fat, too short or tall, shoulders slouched from pressure, hair slightly disarrayed, or too old. They have, for appearance's sake, a perfect body. It will be interesting to see how quickly this ideal is pushed down onto lower-level workers in the next few years, an expression of the hegemonic pressures brought through the culture by all the self-appointed experts on work.

The drives toward individualism and freedom in this culture

provide opportunity for self-expression and growth unfound in and envied by more collectivist societies. We Americans can acquire exceptionally high levels of efficacy and a sense of control over our lives. Part of this good self-feeling is illusory, based upon the erroneous belief in total self-will. We refuse to acknowledge social, historical, cultural, and economic forces upon us, except at times of severe dislocation in the society. In particular, we deny the presence of power and privilege, but insist that success comes by effort alone. The heavy burden accompanying that flush of self-pride is self-deprecation, for no matter how good we seem at any moment, we know it is not enough. We have other errors and sins to expunge. This guilt makes us compliant workers.

Whatever source one looks to for advice on improving one's condition in life, blaming the victim—ourselves—is the underlying theme. Even leftist activists consume much of their political energy in mutual name-calling and accusations that one or the other group is not pure enough. Feminists spend time elaborating on how if only the secretaries would get up from their desks and march out of the offices, the bosses could not help but recognize the value of their work. Black leaders grow impatient with the recalcitrance of slum youth. The individualism transmutes into a policy for the group as a whole. Consequently, the very people who are the stimulus for change, those demanding a reduction in economic inequities, support policies that perpetuate the status quo.

AFFIRMATIVE ACTION REVISITED

The most pervasive and legitimate policy for diminishing work discrimination is affirmative action. Growing out of the discussions of civil-rights activists, feminists, and legislators during the 1960s, it focuses exclusively upon the firm and employer, in its demands that they demonstrate not only a willingness to hire or promote disadvantaged workers, but to encourage and support them as well. On the surface this seems a healthy response to those who would blame the victim and emphasize the development of individual skills. In fact, expression of affirmative action as currently practiced is so flawed that it is of minor value in social change.

According to the model, disadvantaged workers are to be encouraged to seek job mobility, to be transferred to positions from which they can move up in the company, and so on. When two workers are equivalent, the employer is to demonstrate the spirit of equal opportunity by giving the edge to the minority or woman. This "preference" rankles critics the most for its suspiciously radical taint.

An examination of the principle in practice proves that it is strongly conservative in impact. Consider the case of hiring in academia. A major indicator of an individual's ability is the graduate school he or she attended. Harvard is indisputably premier choice, with schools like Stanford, Chicago, Berkeley, Columbia, and Wisconsin close behind. The way academics practice affirmative action—a method many employers elsewhere follow—is to rank candidates for a job. If a woman and a man come from Harvard and have comparable backgrounds, then they will give the job to the woman (if they see it useful to practice affirmative action that year). Over drinks later, they can gripe about how a perfectly good man "lost" the job over a technicality.

Yet this interpretation of affirmative action is incorrect. Given that few women get doctorates from Harvard (because of that institution's history of prejudice and discrimination) very likely any woman who gets a degree from the school has unusual qualities. She is likely to have followed the informal rule of having to work twice as hard as a man to get the same credit. In other words, the man and woman who are alike on paper are not alike at all. They have experienced different demands. The woman has passed a tougher test.

Take this case further. Suppose the committee had a man from Harvard and a working-class Italian from Wisconsin, both with comparable publishing experience and teaching performance. The committee could hire the man from Harvard because he was "better." But is he? When a poor white man's education is limited to state institutions, is it fair to say he is not as qualified as the man who could afford the more expensive private school, especially when it is known that the educational quality of the graduate departments is very high in both cases?

In other words, for affirmative action to be fair in terms of comparing two individuals, a minority and a privileged male, little change will come from demanding that both have enjoyed the same training experiences. Since so few minorities gain the best training, only those that do will benefit from the comparison. In numbers, the change can barely pass a trickle.

The most just comparison would be that between a minority-group member with very good credentials and the privileged male whose credentials are the best. If employers gave minorities the edge in such cases, then more substantial (and equitable) changes would result. However, this would likely lead to revolution in the ranks, because privileged people would claim that those in second place by appearance were second-rate individuals. (As it is, privileged males consider minorities and women with the *best* of credentials to be second rate.)

Another illustration of the conservatism of affirmative action occurs during promotions. For example, women clerical workers are given increasing responsibility over the years while retaining the title "secretary" with its accompanying low pay. To start promoting these women by moving them into low supervisorial roles ignores their accumulated experience. Since fair-play customs dictate that people move up a step at a time, many women will never move to their level of competence (or incompetence).

Furthermore, to start giving women equal opportunity for promotion will leave them at permanent disadvantage with their male peers. Even if they are treated as though their gender were irrelevant, they cannot take in the same lifetime earnings as the men who started out with them but moved ahead more quickly before affirmative action. So again, what seems like a fair policy perpetuates injustices and fails to provide retribution to those who have been injured.

Finally, no matter how good a company's equal-opportunity policy, it will take decades before a firm reaches equity in the distribution of its disadvantaged workers among the better jobs. And those who pass up into the ranks have the onerous task of representing their group in the board rooms. Consequently, their particular personalities will play a larger role in a company's attitude toward affirmative action. If it promotes a woman who for reasons of personal inclination doesn't match˙ well with the top men, they will all be able to blame problems on her being a woman. (Were she a man in the same room, she could blend in with the other men and be known as "a bit difficult.")

If affirmative action were wholeheartedly accepted by all companies and practiced in the traditional sense discussed here (which is the approach consistent with federal guidelines) then it would be some time into the twenty-first century before visible reductions in economic inequality would be apparent. At the present time, only a few workers are likely to benefit in any profound way—primarily young people of all backgrounds just entering management and the professions. The remainder are being sorted out at the hiring posts and locked into jobs with more limited opportunities.

Affirmative action procedures are also susceptible to political influence. Though federal regulations forbid discrimination on the basis of sex, race, religion, national origin, and in some cases, age, when it comes to the collection of statistics, the government has until recently required only data on race and sex. Furthermore, in the daily implementation of regulations, the EEOC and other agency representatives tend to concentrate on the most vocal and organized interest groups. For both business and government, affirmative action in its simplest terms means the advancement of blacks, and since women are second-class in the country, the black male receives the major benefits. The advances of any disadvantaged group are not to be scoffed at, but when one group is singled more than others, natural jealousies lead to divisiveness among people who should be collecting together in a common fight against discrimination.

Currently, Asian-Americans are simply not recognized by government agencies, unions, or employers as a group that is considered disadvantaged. Yet Asians make up a sizable labor force in several large metropolitan areas in the country, so even though they are a tiny minority overall, they are a significant one within the areas where they are employed. In these areas, however, they find themselves now discriminated against because of government rulings about what constitutes a "minority." Until recently in New York or San Francisco, a contractor could satisfy his equal-opportunity compliance requirements without hiring a single Asian-American. Since Asian cultures do not foster the personal traits that are conducive to an outgoing, assertive activism, the local communities have a difficult time getting themselves recognized among the claims of more demonstrative minorities.

Federal requirements also ignore the needs of other groups that have clearly suffered disadvantage. These are the white ethnics, who find themselves crowded into certain blue-collar jobs just as women are crowded into clerical work; people with disabilities, who by name (the Handicapped, the Disabled) are considered incapable of work; persons from geographically depressed areas, such as Appalachian coal mining valleys or Southern Texas barrios; and homosexuals. Of course, to include these categories under the rubric of affirmative action would be to include the vast majority of Americans. How can there be a country where most people suffer economic disadvantage? That, indeed, is the fact the government and employers would have us overlook.

For those fields with a labor glut affirmative action requirements can provoke a reactionary response on the part of male workers. In recent years, graduate schools have continued to produce doctorates in spite of the shrinking college population. They have misled hopeful young academics for the short-run purpose of obtaining cheap labor for research projects and undergraduate teaching. Now, when a hundred white male applicants are rejected, they can blame their fate on the minority or female academic who was hired—even though 98 percent of the white males who applied could not be hired anyway. Also, given the terrible track record of colleges with regard to affirmative action, it is clear that they are still hiring white males most of the time. But whenever one doesn't get hired, he can be told he lost out because of "affirmative action." This has led to considerable bitterness in academia, as letters and editorials in professional organization newsletters will testify. Women and minorities are becoming ready scapegoats for irresponsible administrators.

This university example highlights another difficulty with the affirmative-action approach. The fact is that American colleges today have no way of putting large numbers of women and minorities on their faculties because not enough in the past have earned Ph.D.'s. If American colleges were to hire every black Ph.D., active or retired, draining them from government, business, and other institutions, they would find themselves with an average of three blacks per institution. Yet white male academics are running scared.

The fears of these men remind us that the issue of equality threatens the ego structure of those trained to believe in superiority as part of the natural order. Men who have been raised to be distrustful of others, to depend only upon themselves, to repress emotions and sensual needs, must feel inadequate in the presence of others from society who seem to enjoy themselves on the basis of opposite principles. These men's fear of loss is real, and those working to implement affirmative action can ill ignore the perceptions and defenses of those who feel pushed aside. This is all the more reason to promote minorities in clusters, rather than have one or two vulnerable to the machinations and attacks of insecure coworkers. The process of change affects both those being promoted and their new peers, though often only the psychological needs of the former are considered in company plans.

Although affirmative-action policy is fraught with difficulties, its presence on the law books has definitely opened opportunities for scattered groups of workers. At present, enforcement appears to be a lottery, with employers willing to take their chances that their names won't be pulled for review and litigation. An undergrowth of countermoves to blunt the effectiveness of plans lies thick in some organizations. (In the next chapter I shall address some practical managerial tactics to improve implementation.)

Yet no matter how effectively affirmative action is enforced, it cannot produce major change, because it ignores the major sources of inequity. The problem is that equal opportunity as presently conceptualized ignores the profound cultural—and

ultimately political-economic—reasons for inequality. The
federal regulations do not ask employers to provide meaningful work to all, nor to open up channels between jobs so workers can be more mobile, nor to redesign their organizations so
that many workers get a liveable wage rather than a few enjoy
lush benefits. They do not address the economic costs of providing good work for employees in the market economy as
against those in the corporations. What they do is reinforce the
idea that work is a world of a few winners and many losers,
that the best individuals win. All the government is asking is
that the rules be a bit fairer to people who by definition were
never allowed to win in the past. Their dice are slightly loaded
now, though not as heavily as those of the privileged. A few of
the newcomers will win, and will be able to announce, "We did
it all ourselves. Women's lib had nothing to do with it."

Chapter 11

A New Primer for Affirmative Action

Men have always had the right to determine whether the incremental increase in remuneration for strenuous, dangerous, obnoxious, boring, or unromantic tasks is worth the candle. The promise of Title VII is that women are now on an equal footing.

Weeks vs. Southern Bell Telephone and Telegraph

The most important measure of an Affirmative Action Program is its RESULTS.

U.S. Equal Employment Opportunity Commission

In the ongoing debates over affirmative action, many people talk from the top of their heads. Some assert simply that "employers discriminate," a statement that describes the situation rather than illuminates it. Others point their fingers and say, "Employers are racist and sexist," thus implying that the maintenance of white male supremacy is the primary and conscious intent of managers. Countering these claims are the employers, who respond: "Affirmative action will disrupt work too much and be too costly"—a curious response, since bosses are constantly making decisions that disrupt work places and cause unusual expenses, in the name of long-run profit or productivity.

To complicate matters, each side speaks with partial reason. Certainly bigots exist in the management world, and they lean upon their bigotry as the guiding paradigm in all worker relations. Or, in the whitewashed language of one EEOC report, "There are simply large numbers of average WASP males in above-average jobs who do not wish to share them with above-average minority group members or WASP women." And for tight-resource work places, particularly those in the

market or service economy, the development of an affirmative-action unit can threaten survival.

On the other hand, when looking over the range of employers and their attempts at equal opportunity, one sees that well-
intentioned managements do exist. When the EEOC studied
equal-employment changes in large public utilities, it found
considerable contrasts.[1] This industry utilizes primarily blue-
collar workers who receive their training on the job. Consequently, the claim that unqualified women and minority employees cannot be found does not apply to their hiring. Nonetheless, in 1971, public utilities ranked last among the
twenty-three largest industries in the U.S. in the employment
of blacks. However, the EEOC found that each utility was
unique in its exclusion of women and blacks from hiring or
promotion, and in its implementation of equal opportunity
programs. For example, five years following the federal regulations against work discrimination, Pacific Gas and Electric had
no affirmative action program for women, and, though located
near a large Spanish-speaking work force, had done nothing to
recruit in that community. A vice-president of the company
testifying before the EEOC knew neither of the existence of a
major Spanish-speaking recruitment organization, nor had he
any data on the Spanish-speaking work force within his firm.
In contrast, managers at Consolidated Edison of New York had
established a strong equal-opportunity program. Based upon
research into their hiring practices, they identified access to
jobs as the major stumbling block for minority workers. Consequently, they developed a vigorous and effective community
outreach program and modified their hiring standards to eliminate latent racial bias. The problem for affirmative action advocates is to ensure that cases like Consolidated Edison become
more prevalent than those of PG&E.

When activists and lawmakers developed the federal equal-
opportunity regulations, they operated on a naive view of management, one presuming that company decision-makers can
directly and readily implement policy. Anyone who has ever
walked into an office or bureaucracy knows how absurd this
view is. It is silly to think that the execution of federal guidelines is never hampered by recalcitrant supervisors, red tape,

snafus, and other foul-ups. As business leaders are increasingly realizing, organizations have a life of their own that does not match the old rational-actor model of management. Work settings are not the military (as if the military itself were a worthwhile model of efficiency) or a football team (which loses many games as well as wins them). Nor is management a science, whereby the administrator combines this technique with that one to achieve a certain level of productivity. At the same time, work places are influenced by the culture of the society in which they are embedded. When that culture is racist and sexist, then it blinds managers from seeing all the opportunities open to them. Once these influences within and without the organization are considered, then novel and practical applications for affirmative-action policy emerge.

PERSONNEL FALLACIES

Since there is a long tradition of assigning jobs by social characteristics, it is easy for employers to rationalize that workers fit some positions like pegs to holes, only one kind fitting well. Although "secretary" was initially a masculine occupation, it transformed into a female ghetto, accumulating the accoutrements of the female role, such as making coffee or performing personal services for a boss, and other tasks that make the job unappealing to men. Implicit in their view is the notion that the work group should be homogeneous. Supporting myths here include "A man doesn't work well with a woman boss," "Blacks and whites don't mix well together on the same team," and "Women are happiest when working with other women."

It is not necessarily so that personnel people say to themselves, "This black belongs on janitorial service," or "This woman is good only as a file clerk." While blatant cases of racism or sexism doubtless occur, employers are, after all, good Americans who as school children also pledged "equality and justice for all." Consequently they need a rationale for their decisions. The prevalent solution is to practice what economist Lester Thurow calls "statistical discrimination."[2]

According to this theory, employers examine the performance of workers from various groups and estimate their overall human capital. For example, suppose an insurance company looks over its sales trainee records and discovers that on the average more black trainees dropped out than white trainees. The difference can be small—a matter of three or four more blacks per hundred applicants failing to complete the program. The size of the difference is not relevant, because an accountant's mind tends to choose the least-expensive solution to executive decisions. Given this knowledge, the employer will then find it most expedient and efficient, by his model, to select white applicants for the program and accept black ones only when the supply of whites is low.

This means an applicant will be judged by the average characteristics of the group he or she represents. Jobs and earnings are determined by peers. If the company's earlier attempt to place a women on the all-male sales force failed, then no new women can hope to break into that department. If the several young men hired by a previously all-white company quit much sooner than the average white worker, then black applicants will be labelled as potential quitters, and less valuable as workers.

Thurow tends to blame the victim with this theory. For example, he argues that because more women than men leave the labor force, employers will not rationally want to invest in women, and every woman worker, however loyal, must suffer. So long as any member of a group has "undesired characteristics," then all members of the group will be viewed as defective. This reasoning even creeps into activist rhetoric. There were speeches in which Martin Luther King advised black people to "clean themselves up" and behave politely so they could be more acceptable to whites. And though early feminists urged women to drop constraining underwear and dress, by 1978 the magazine *Ms.* allowed that bleached hair and stylish clothes had a purpose in the work world.

Thurow's individualism favors employers in another way. In the insurance example, company executives can ignore whether the black dropout rate was due to features of the training program or the company itself. Also, the female dropout rate in this country reflects the nature of women's work, not the quality of women workers. Assembly-line jobs, waitressing, salesclerking, clerical work, and nursing are not positions that have well-paid career trajectories; men in these jobs have similarly high quit rates. With many women workers carrying two jobs (even if one is unpaid domestic labor), their rejection of poorly-paid work is completely rational. Why should they remain loyal to an employer who offers little return? The benefit of low-level work, if there is one, is the ability to drop out temporarily at any point and not damage one's employment record, for there will always be a comparable job in the area. Indeed, employers can in these cases claim they are doing women a favor by not paying them well and placing them in jobs of little long-term consequence. And many women can buy this rationalization—until the day they are divorced, widowed, or realize they will always have to support themselves.

Obviously, the statistical discrimination procedure is costly in that it arbitrarily excludes large numbers of workers who could do as good a job, if not a better job than those who are accepted. When only men are considered qualified for a position, and are hired first, then a range of men, from competent to mediocre to inept, can be placed before women are given priority. Thus employers pay in the long run by excluding the talented from other groups. As a result, our work organizations are often frustrating to everyone. Inept men in managerial ranks misdirect and misguide underlings, and complicate the lives of their skillful male peers. Talented women, inhibited from demonstrating their abilities, grow angry and fierce toward coworkers and clients. Bright men in laboring positions sabotage machines.

As many contemporary career guides correctly (if cynically) emphasize, craft, dedication, and ethically-based behavior will not necessarily be rewarded at work—appearances, connections, and petty politics matter at least as much, even more in specific cases. The hypocrisy and contradiction between American rhetoric and reality are apparent to all but the neurotic, who suffer in their blindness. The best man, or best woman for that matter, doesn't get the best job.

This determination to keep work groups homogeneous itself

reflects irrational needs of management. In a time when top administrators are dying their hair, getting face lifts, and hiring fashion consultants to keep their jobs, there is little incentive for lower-level managers to integrate their ranks.[3] This cloning is an unnecessarily defensive and inappropriate attempt to ensure trust and consensus in decision-making. Yet behavioral science has well established that homogeneous groups are prone to insularity, narrowmindedness, and self-serving prejudice—hardly the best qualities for solving critical work organization problems.

It is at this level that the personalities of the men who lead our work places matter. If these men are disdainful and frightened of their softer qualities, then they are not going to want to work with people who are as comfortable with intuition, receptivity, and interpersonal sensitivity as with calculation, assertiveness, and production control.[4] If they think of women as sexual objects, and think of less-educated, less-polished men as inferior, then they cannot make humane decisions. The moral solution is also the practical one, but managers have not been shown the cost-inefficiency of their ways to understand this point.

Statistical discrimination is popular because it appears an easy solution to an employer's most difficult problem: the placement of the worker to job. Modern personnel practices aren't very effective. Seldom do job interviewers have the careful, lengthy training needed to become a sensitive and unbiased evaluator of an individual's potential. Persons untrained in test administration and interpretation apply the devices incorrectly and haphazardly. In one 1979 study of the San Diego area, employers almost unanimously agreed that their sole basis for hiring was the interview, that an unfavorable personal appearance could discredit the best resumé and vice versa. One major corporation told the researcher that it never hired anyone who hadn't freshly shined shoes.[5]

The fact is that people with qualities at odds with WASP society are no greater employment risks than those who fit the mold.[6] The bearded man with an arrest record for civil disobedience, the unwed mother of three, the young Chicano with a poor credit record, or the older woman dressed in secondhand clothes cannot be assumed to be less valuable employees than those who appear well-dressed, have no regional accent and know how to cover up such discrediting evidence as an unhappy marriage, a dependence upon liquor, or sheer laziness. Human vice distributes evenly throughout the population: each individual job applicant will bear a bundle of strong and weak character traits. The only "risk" is that disadvantaged people will not be understood sensitively, intelligently evaluated for employment, validly tested for interests and skills, properly oriented to assume responsibility on the job, and encouraged to develop self-esteem, confidence, and trust. Employers lose out on these "risks" daily.

The exclusion of good workers from jobs affects all levels of the organization, but nowhere is it held more fiercely today than in the mythology of the good manager. He is aggressive, competitive, firm, and just one who eschews visible use of intuition and expression of feeling. This expectation applies better to some stereotypes in our society than others—to men better than women, to whites than blacks, to Anglo-Saxons than southern Mediterraneans. A woman who behaves assertively will be called a bitch; a woman who expresses emotion will be called weak. Either way she cannot satisfy the managerial ideal.

Ironically, this preference does not seem to have any relationship to decision-making skill.[7] Studies of leadership effectiveness have failed to uncover any consistent pattern in personality, physical attributes, or aptitudes that consistently distinguish good managers from bad ones. In fact, many styles of leadership exist. Some managers develop close, intimate, quasi-familial ties with their subordinates; others hold to rigid narrow styles of interaction. Both may stimulate the same amount of productivity. Similarly, there are business leaders who in autobiographical comment attribute their achievement to careful, rational calculation, and others who thank their sixth sense or hunch work.

In other words, contemporary managers are clinging to a fallacious model of leadership when selecting and evaluating new decision makers. Doing so allows them to gain some sense of security—the others in administration are most likely to be men of the same background as themselves. But this can result in great foolishness for a society where the clientele, whether of stores, hospitals, schools, or government agencies, are going to include people of minority races and ethnic groups, Spanish-speaking, the elderly and youth, women and people with disabilities. How can the needs of such a diverse body be met by a group of men who have experienced a dissimilar, often privileged lifestyle?

For companies and firms without direct clienteles, the managerial model is inefficient in another way. Because the decision makers are of one kind, they will tend to look at problems from the same perspective. They will be as blind men describing an elephant all on the basis of the same approach, such as grabbing at the tail. Thus modern administrators sacrifice creativity and ingenuity in their determination to preserve what Wilbur Moore has aptly coined company life, "homosexual reproduction."[8]

ORGANIZATIONAL BOTTLENECKS

Looking over equal-opportunity surveys of banks, insurance companies, stores, universities, industries, and other employers, the obvious emerges: work places are not alike. Some corporations value a public service image, hence actively incorporate the latest public need, be it ecology, conservation, or civil rights, into its decision making. Others pose a defensive, you-have-to-sue-us-first attitude and hire a cadre of lawyers to fight possible complaints and court cases. Many wallow in a grey area, bemused and confused by conflicting federal regulations and a contentious public. There's no predicting an employer's behavior on a case-by-case basis.

While no one employer may be like another, all firms eventually exhibit similar pathologies in their affirmative-action activities. EEOC investigations and hearings repeat a litany of ineffective procedures, many of which occur in companies where management appears to have made a strong, determined commitment to change its past discriminatory ways. Why should ill-meaning and well-meaning firms in time produce equally useless practices? The answer rests with the nature of organizations and human communications processes.[9]

A key defect in many firms is the location of the affirmative-action office within a weak position in the organization. A typical example is the placement of an Equal Employment Opportunity Officer within either Personnel or Public Relations, neither of which are on the direct line to top-level management. Or there may be an Affirmative Action Committee, a common occurrence in universities and professional schools, to which departments must refer hiring decisions, but which those departments may be able to overrule. These placements leave equal opportunity officers with little authority, and often few resources. They can become nuisance appendages to the organization that everyone must get around.

For example, in college teaching, all a department need do is establish on paper ahead of time a set of qualifications that match someone it would like to hire, go through the motions of a public applicant search, and then establish that their choice is superior to any other applicants. The "buddy system," whereby jobs are obtained through personal connections, continues unabated, though at the additional cost of many hours of paperwork. Or, in firms where department supervisors have less leeway in job descriptions, the affirmative action directives appear to be intrusions on personal authority. If a blue-collar supervisor can't hire his best friend's cousin, whom he knows to be a good kid, because he has to take on some minorities, then he develops doubts and disenchantment about his role.

In an ideal management world, supervisors and middle-management people would be directed to cooperate with affirmative-action officers, and would be held accountable to follow through on directives. This seldom occurs. In fact, companies often purposely withhold information from their own employees. In one study of ten major corporations with affirmative-action programs, the line management was generally ignorant as to whether the firm had a program, what its policies were, or what the timetables were. Half the managers said that the company stated sex preferences in its advertisements, when in fact this was not the case. These ten companies were described by the EEOC as actively committed at the top managerial level to the pursuit of equal opportunity for women. Clearly that commitment had not reached those employees who had day-to-day control over the implementation of policies.

Some employers set up equal-opportunity units and then fail to provide the facilities for the information gathering and analysis that is required for thoughtful, sensitive programs. As the EEOC reports reiterate, "Record keeping is not automated in the firm and each unit keeps its own personnel records," or "No detailed statistical data have been prepared in the firm to measure EEO performance." Ironically, the employers that maintain this data are the most likely to be able to prepare a solid defense in case of a lawsuit. Ignorance is no defense—though it may seem more comfortable than facing the hard facts of work discrimination within the company.

It is noteworthy that the deficiency in data collection may be blamed partly on the EEOC itself. Its compliance personnel, who visit employers and consult in the development of programs, and review programs periodically, are not consistent in their demands. One consultant may tell the company to focus upon a particular minority, sex, or religious group that is of special interest to her. Another may come in a year later and ask for data on recruitment, rejection rates, promotion lists, and so on. A third may ask for only the most basic data.

Furthermore, the government has been naive in assuming that all employers have the staff and resources to develop data banks. Federal government workers spend their lives compiling reports of the type company affirmative-action offices are to fill out. Though it may seem easy to them, the paperwork may be beyond the understanding of staff in smaller companies, where activity is less bureaucratized. Consequently, in some firms affirmative action may in fact be exceptionally costly and unproductive because the staff does not know the most effective procedures for preparing the data.

Given lack of good base information, the equal-opportunity programs themselves can have obvious weaknesses. The EEOC discovered one company in which a goal of 20 percent women for management had been established. The company claimed this goal was based upon a survey of university placement officers in the area with respect to the supply of potential women applicants for the firm. As the EEOC pointed out, considerably more than 20 percent of college majors are women, so the goal was far too low. Another example is the southern utility company that decided its main emphasis should be on the promotion of minority workers. But it had few minority workers, and made no efforts to hire more. So the plan was a sham, unable to affect the work life of minorities in the community.

Employers also fail to take obvious actions. Outside of posting a notice in ads or in the personnel office that they are "an equal opportunity employer," they do not inform workers of their rights. A union may be a source of some workers, and may share control over personnel practices, and yet not be included in program planning. Although it would seem reasonable to expect a regular review of affirmative-action programs, management often does not require such of the administrators.

The federal regulatory approach is weak because it motivates by threat, and thus places managers on the defensive. Since they know that the government itself has not implemented forceful and visible affirmative-action policies, they may decide that it is worth chancing a lawsuit and facing the problem when and if it arises. The media's emphasis upon violations also hinders the development of useful programs. Firms with creative, successful equal-opportunity projects don't make the front pages of the newspapers—or the business pages, for that matter. The government has failed to offer positive models to employers to help them realize the spirit of the law.

As a consequence, most companies concentrate their equal-opportunity activities in two areas: reaching out into minority communities to obtain more hires, and buying ads to broadcast their social conscience. But the spirit of the law requires that hiring procedures be reevaluated, that current employees' careers be reviewed and opportunities given to those who have been affected by past discriminatory policies, that wage and salary schedules be redrawn where necessary, that benefits be equalized, and that union contracts be revised to treat all employees fairly. Furthermore, the thrust of company policies has been on racial-minority men to the neglect of women of any race.

Simply adding new faces to low-level jobs does not correct the injustices suffered by present workers. Promoting a few minorities or women to positions of responsibility leaves them vulnerable as tokens. They will stand out in the office or work group, and by their very visibility be more subject to scrutiny and evaluation. The token worker is handicapped by definition because he or she must run twice as hard in order to be considered competent by peers. Even then, equal treatment in the way of future promotions or pay raises is not certain, since companies may want to avoid antagonizing previously privileged males.

Successful firms show an awareness of the complexity of the equal-opportunity problem. One company holds its middle management and supervisors accountable for complying with federal regulations, and includes an evaluation of their performance in this area in regular reviews of work. Obviously, when a possible promotion or raise is dependent upon meeting company timetables, middle managers are going to find ways to meet the timetables. Another company has recognized that clerical jobs have become a female ghetto, and to upgrade their image has openly recruited male typists and stenographers, finding large numbers of qualified men from among veterans (who learned the necessary skills in the military). Other employers are learning that they have been much too narrow in their listing of job qualifications. For example, when AT&T wanted to place more women in management, it developed assessment programs to identify workers who might otherwise have been ignored because they lacked the paper qualifications. Workers were given problems and experiences simulating the real demands of managerial decision-making. In repeated studies, Bell has found that the proportions of potential men and women candidates are identical, and furthermore, that these diagnostic procedures are more valid in identifying managerial material overall.[10] Other employers are discovering that the time and staff given over the establishment of career development counseling pays off in the long run, because employees who are unaware of their capabilities or who believe little advancement is possible because of their personal characteristics are paid attention to and encouraged to increase their aspirations.

The crux of the failure of equal-opportunity programming is bad managment. Whether this is the result of intention or of ineptness is besides the point. Organizations are ultimately the creation of managers. This is why college presidents, corporation executives, hospital administrators, and factory owners are rewarded with high prestige and material goods—they are given an extraordinary responsibility, the invention of social structure.

The skeleton for a well-managed equal-opportunity program would include at least the following components:[11]

1. *Corporate Blue Letter.* A strong equal-employment policy must have the unified endorsement of all the chief officers of the firm. A forceful, unambiguous statement of policy should be distributed in a widely visible manner: memo, bulletin board, in-house publication, employee manual. As the program develops, management should disseminate statements on related topics, such as the condemnation of sexual harassment, the guarantee of safe work conditions for all employees, or the encouragement of career development.

2. *Realistic Policy Development.* Unfortunately, EEOC accounting procedures encourage a mindless quota-setting. A wise policy is process-oriented, built upon flow models over time rather than balance sheet pictures.[12] It requires hard data on the local labor market, job turnover, promotional timetables, and some computer time, but the effort pays off in terms of clear, achievable goals that will make sense to workers, management, and the government.

3. *Avoiding the "Token" Problem.* Employers should promote women and minorities in batches, not singly, so that individuals are not left isolated in departments as the sole representatives of their groups. Similarly, care should be taken to avoid turning certain departments into managerial ghettos, e.g., personnel departments for women, equal-opportunity departments for minorities. For this reason, a forward-

moving program will place its first promotions in the departments where they would be least expected, such as financial or sales divisions, and later place in areas where women and minorities have always had some entree.

4. *Management Training Sessions.* A special educational program should be designed to explain the firm's position on equal opportunity in full. The emphasis should be that bias is unproductive both for the firm and the individual, and that its practice can cost the employee his or her career. Outside consultants can provide the most efficient and effective programs here; they are especially valuable for their ability to provide a supportive, nonthreatening environment where white male workers can face their fears and defenses.[13]

5. *Branch Meetings.* Training and information programs at the department and branch level are crucial to ensure that middle management understands firm policy. Communications should be encouraged from this group for additions and modifications in procedures, as these are the people most involved in day-to-day implementation.

6. *Employee Surveys.* Ask outside consultants to interview and survey employees in confidentiality as to their perceptions of blockages in the organization. This survey should go beyond the surface activities of wages and promotion, to such issues as time scheduling, child care, sexual harassment, informal racist patterns, and so forth. The results should be made available to all workers, not just management. Based on this knowledge, implement new procedures rather than sit and wait for individuals to press complaints.

7. *Establishment of Supportive Investigative and Grievance Procedures.* Situations surrounding equal opportunity complaints are often complex, complicated, and emotionally colored. Consequently, EEO staff must be sophisticated in the understanding of organizational behavior, social psychology, and the cultural backgrounds of workers. Given historical conditions, it is likely that most cases or complaints will be valid. The humane firm must be open to processing complaints and apply this knowledge toward the creation of more equitable policy. At the same time, the organization has a right to be protected from the exploitation of those rare, yet present work-

ers who will twist policy for self-serving and venal ends. A stepwise procedure process with little red tape is best—one that begins with informal solution, then brings in a higher level administrator, and finally goes to the EEO department. Perhaps the most productive procedure for both complainant and company would rely upon outside arbitrators and consultants, rather than leave final power within upper management. Managers and supervisors should be informed that any harassment of complainants is coercive, a violation of law as well as of human dignity.

8. *Orienting Employees.* All new employees should be advised of equal opportunity policy and rights. Stemming from the recognition that this is a new situation for most workers, an ideal program would include human relations training or counseling to help workers develop the skills and attitudes to act in non-prejudicial ways.

9. *Meeting the Needs of Both Sides During Grievances.* Both complainant and supervisor will be in vulnerable psychological states once a grievance is formally charged. The needs of both have been well-documented; there is the fear of job loss, of retributions, loss of self-worth, and the firm must guarantee a sense of security to these persons. Instead of either automatically protecting or punishing the manager or coworker, a humane firm will offer counseling and resocialization. Companies provide alcohol therapy and other services to employees; they can just as well help them to develop more open, tolerant ways of relating with people different from themselves.

10. *Establish a Disciplinary Agenda.* Management should publicize and implement a clearcut sequence of sanctions toward workers who inhibit, disrupt, or violate equal-opportunity policies. A sample paradigm is:

1. Consult informally and place a memo on file.
2. Issue a formal warning.
3. Require counseling or remedial consultation.
4. Issue a low performance rating.
5. Withhold a transfer or work assignment.
6. Put on probation.
7. Fire.

When counseling and deterrents fail, fire the worker. Not

doing so leaves the firm open to lawsuits, bad press, and poor worker relations.

Ultimately, none of these changes can solve the basic problem, which is the organization of work into hierarchical units with blocked channels of mobility. Nor do these changes come without disruptions of the work culture, conflicts, and disagreements. But the long-run payoffs of increased heterogeneity throughout the organization should prove even in the accountant's mind that affirmative action, when developed with humaneness and wisdom, is sensible from the point of view of profits.

EQUAL PAY: A REINTERPRETATION

Though companies can do more to open up the higher rungs of job ladders to disadvantaged groups, large numbers of people will remain in deadend positions. Consequently, pay inequalities will remain. Another managerial solution for decreasing inequality would be to reevaluate salary determinations. A high-school dropout male earns more money on the average than a college-graduate female; it is odd that the worst men's jobs would pay better than the best of women's. Much of the current salary discrimination can be linked directly to longstanding patterns in American business.

According to the American Dream, a person's earnings depend upon the job he or she acquires and not directly upon personal characteristics, such as sex or race. Skin color matters then only during the actual competition for job opportunities. In the classical world of economics, employers use wages to control the market by raising or lowering them to attract or dissuade applicants.

The deficiencies of this approach are obvious. For one, about a fourth of all jobs are controlled by union contracts with wages set according to clearcut guidelines, so that a journeyman apprentice carpenter knows precisely how her wages will increase once she passes her training requirements. And by controlling entry of applicants into a field, the union assures that competition for jobs will be kept at a level favorable to its interests. Carpenters earn their pay in boom times and bust (although the hours of employment naturally vary and affect individual income). Second, about a fourth of jobs come under local, county, state, and national government, and typically enjoy the benefits of preestablished civil service rankings. Thus, while there is a surfeit of government workers in some agencies today, they are not paid less in order to deplete the job rosters. Third, skilled workers who are unemployed do not bid to accept lower wages and take away jobs from others. For example, the increasing number of unemployed teachers cannot offer to teach a class for $1,000 a year less than the present job occupant. All they can do is offer to take part-time or temporary work, to which benefits are seldom attached. Many colleges around the country today are benefiting by hiring highly skilled academics for brief-term appointments at cut-rate wages. (In fact, they are seeking to eliminate tenure so that they can have a transient teaching staff at low expense.)

The teaching example illustrates another defect in the classical model. A teacher cannot easily transfer to a well-paying job, since job requirements will not give credit for the years of teaching experience. The teacher with ten years' experience will have considerable skills for sales or management—public speaking ability, organizational adeptness, persuasive powers, and leadership traits, to name a few. Yet he will be thought unqualified to enter other than a training slot in a corporation because he doesn't fit their narrow definition of the job definition. His being attracted to and qualified for a well-paying job will not lead to his appointment. Finally, some jobs which are greatly in demand—consider, for example, the burgeoning need for middle-level clerical workers in the past two decades—have not been accompanied by a comparable increase in wages. By excluding women from other occupations, firms have been able to ensure a steady availability of workers at the typewriters and duplicating machines. Wages have not been relevant to controlling the market in this case.

In recent years economists have agreed that the classical view of wages does not make sense. Consequently, when asked why women can buy fewer eggs for the breakfast table, the experts will answer that women are "marginal workers" or "not in the primary labor force." When government spokespersons answer a reporter's questions about the low incomes of blacks, they will point to the low-valued work being done. The implication is clear: women and minorities earn less because they aren't doing anything worthwhile. Men feed the furnace that drives the economy, while women and minorities stand outside and sweep up a few of the ashes.

The experts have hit the problem precisely, though they don't recognize so. Privileged men make more money because those in power value their work more. Gloria Steinem has said that if men menstruated they would brag about how long and how much and cite menstruation as proof that only men could serve in the Army or occupy political office.[14] If they did domestic chores, like the New Guinea highlands men, they would doubtless compete for political status on the basis of the fine quality of their crocheting.

Sex-segregated work is not inherently unjust. Anthropologists have found societies where the twain of husbands and wives never meet, yet each respects the labor of the other. What matters is a culture's evaluation of the labor. In the United States, this would mean that schoolteachers are as valued for their instruction of children as managers are for their work in facilitating production, that nurses are as respected for their physical and emotional treatment of the patient as are doctors for their technical manipulations. Such a notion can only sound radical, for it challenges deeply set beliefs about the value of labor.

The history of these attitudes lies in the pages of personnel management books, particularly the chapters about pay setting. As late as the fifties, these sources advised higher salaries for men because they headed households, and less for women because they didn't need the money as much. These erroneous maxims are still present today in the salary scales of every firm.

Not all companies follow custom in developing their pay scales. In the more "modern" firms, the approach is to assess the content of the job and apply a numerical value based on such factors as the knowledge and skills required, accountability for one's actions, mental demands, and such special working conditions as hazards or physical effort. These scores are then broken into salary ranges.[15]

Yet these methods are not immune to racist or sexist interference. Clearly, if there is a long history of prejudice toward certain people, then the jobs they hold are prone to underevaluation. Job classifiers and evaluators are predominantly white males, who would be most unusual if they did not want to give their own kind special treatment.

When evaluation systems are examined for hidden biases, a variety of systematic errors appear, which have been best documented in the case of sex:

- Men lift heavy objects occasionally in their work, while women lift light ones frequently. The total effort may be similar, but job evaluations ignore this possibility, and count only the weight of the object. We are more impressed when the weightlifter thrusts a few heavy bells over his head in the competition ring, not when he makes quick, repeated lifts of lighter loads during exhausting practice periods.
- Women are more often assigned to jobs requiring a visual scan for defects in materials, and the ability to decide quickly whether the objects meet quality-control standards. This is how the bad apples, fish, and candy get sorted from the batches. These skills are discounted in evaluation systems as trivial.
- Males are responsible for property, females for persons. In the United States, property protection takes precedence. For example, the Department of Labor until 1978 judged a child-care attendant to be equivalent to a parking-lot attendant, a nurse midwife less skilled than a hotel clerk.
- On paper, men's white-collar jobs call for more decision making and responsibility, although in fact they may rely upon their female clerks and aides to formulate the decisions. The department head has the responsibility to plan and execute his budget, but his secretary may do the job and type his name on the front page. He gets the reward.
- Women's jobs are characterized by more interruptions and simultaneous processing. For example, secretaries must not only type accurately, but do so in spite of phone and per-

sonal requests. Nurses must do charts, administer medicines, and keep order on the ward while being available to the immediate demands of patients, doctors, and visitors. These special work conditions are not given additional credit in evaluations.
· Women's jobs elicit interpersonal skills; men's, physical skills. Evaluation systems reward brawn and ignore tact.
· When requiring other than a normal daytime forty-hour week, men's work is compensated with additional pay. Women's work, such as nursing, is not.
· Male jobs provide on-the-job training, which is counted into evaluation scales. Female jobs require that the applicants come to work skilled; not only are these skills undervalued ("anyone can type"), but subsequent on-the-job training (learning how to type special formats; handling customer complaints) is overlooked.
· The unpleasant work conditions of men's jobs, because they are so dramatic, are counted. You can't ignore the heat and fumes of the steel mill. The hazards of women's work—extended sitting, the continual clatter of office machines—are not noticed.

If men and women's jobs were evaluated equivalently, with women's skills and special work demands being attended to in a sensible, reasonable way, then men would still have a slight edge in salary, though not a great one. This is because all dangerous work in the United States is men's work.

The effects of revamped wage evaluations can be seen in the recent experience of the state of Washington. In the early 1970s the state reevaluated the pay scales of its high administrative jobs, with the result that many workers in these positions moved up to a higher pay scale. Lower-level workers in the government, predominantly women, asked that the same reevaluation be done for their work. The results suggested the need for a total restructure of salary ladders.[16]

At that time, traffic guides, mostly male, monitored the parking of cars and collection of fees. The only requirement for the job was a valid driver's license. This job earned $634 a month. The entry-level clerical job, Secretary III, required the ability to type 50 or more words per minute with no more than one error, take shorthand or machine transcription, manage a small office, supervise other clerical employees, and perform other tasks. This job, for all its skill requirements, brought in $650—just a few dollars more a month. A comparable male job, that of construction coordinator, required two years of college, the ability to read blueprints, and to oversee minor construction jobs. This position brought in $1,092.

A consulting firm was hired to rate these and other jobs according to such components as the knowledge and skills required, mental demands, accountability, and working conditions. According to their evaluations, Traffic Guide was assigned 89 points, Secretary III, 210, and Construction Coordinator, 217. In other words, the secretary should be earning much more money for her performance.

The consulting firm concluded that any action to achieve equitable salaries between women and men in state government would require adoption of a procedure such as the one they suggested. Little happened afterward. The governor authorized an update of the study and a small budget appropriation to begin implementation of the results. Then Dixie Lee Ray came into office and deleted this item. Although she had accepted the same consultant's earlier study on administrative jobs, she argued that their later work was not valid. An independent investigator of the Washington case concluded that the policy failed for the explicit reason that it was argued to improve the lot of women, because similar systems have been successfully introduced only when the payoff to female workers was not mentioned as one of the benefits.

It may be difficult to convince employers of the value of establishing more equitable pay scales. Since many workers, such as traffic guides, would not want their pay to go down, then large numbers of workers, such as secretaries, must be given jumps in salary. In the state of Washington, approximately half of all employees would find their salary scale changed. The estimated total annual cost would be over 37 million dollars, hardly a figure pleasing in these days of taxpayer revolts.

These costs are deceiving. If women and minorities were

paid according to their worth, however broadly that were measured, then they would contribute more to the productivity of the economy as consumers, as well as significantly decrease the welfare burden on the public. This pay equity would have long-term effects in that all dependents of these workers would benefit as well. If Americans do not want to give up the competition and ranking of the labor market (and there are good reasons not to shelve it completely), then they can still make a commitment to equality by asking that historically erroneous bases for salary assignment be overthrown. And the wise manager, who realizes that the good of the business depends upon the good of the general economy, has much to gain by anticipating these demands.

Chapter 12

Possible Dreams

When people talk about equality and human dignity, they really want acceptance—I shy away from the word love, but that is what it is—in spite of all differences.
Walter A. Weisskopf, "The Dialectics of Equality,"
                    The "Inequality" Controversy

The arc of the universe is long, but it bends toward justice.

                              Martin Luther King, Jr.

If many of the popular cures for eliminating discrimination are merely Band-Aids or salves that ultimately irritate the situation more than they help it, then what is to be done? The need is to develop a praxis that attacks the germ of the problem. So long as society designs a work structure where people must battle one another for positions of dignity, affluence, and power, then women, men, blacks, orientals, the middle-aged, and the young will compete for the spoils. So long as people are taught that some jobs are dirty, disgusting, and disreputable, they will struggle in their rush to avoid such tasks and push others back to handle them. If people are raised to believe that they are autonomous and in control of their own destinies, when in fact their paths at birth are as clearly mapped out as an astrologer's chart, then they will pass their lives in bitterness and shame.

It is tempting to offer a visionary response, to point to the dimensions of a society where lives have been spent according to principles other than individualism, competition, and hierarchy. This picture of the future is not a novel one; radicals have painted it for over a century. Yet in my own experience, with its narrow, day-to-day, personal view of life, such depictions leave me uncomfortable and frustrated, for I see a large gap between the world as currently constructed and the world that in my realist's eyes will not come about in this lifetime (unless through violent revolution).

The question of most interest for me is how those of us who desire change can move, given our limited resources and power. What can one person today do to feel he or she has contributed to a better life for her descendants? The proposals offered here are best seen as examples of policies that can operate to direct the society toward a system based more on mutual respect and cooperation than on invidious comparisons. They are offered as paradigms for those who may be able to develop them further in considering practical possibilities for social change.

Underlying these recommendations is a model for a new work ethos:

- Rather than fit people into a lifelong slot, they will be trained to be multifunctional and adaptable. In a small, stable, rural society with clear-cut jobs, it makes sense to raise particular people to become the town blacksmith, doctor, or minister; but in a society structured upon change and flux, such demands are wasteful. The chemist who is up to date at twenty-five, but grows out of date by the age of forty-five should be able to change careers. Even professions requiring long training, such as medicine, law, or engineering, should accept mid-life students for the value of their experience and wisdom. When society does push some persons toward high specialization, it should also guarantee retraining if their skills become obsolete (as a result of rapid technological developments) or undesirable (as a result of politics or economic demands).
- All adults are viewed as employable, with the potential to do many jobs. The bizarre notion of the economists and policy makers, that 5 percent unemployment is a full employment economy, must be tossed out. We cannot afford the waste of bright people with physical disabilities who are left to languish alone in their apartments day after day; we cannot ignore the desires of the developmentally disabled to be free of institutions and self-supporting. Nor can we tolerate the shameful neglect of poor youth and the tacit acceptance by

those in power that this group of Americans can be labelled as permanently unemployable by virtue of birth. Extending this idea to presently-employed workers, persons will not be judged solely on the basis of their past. Because a woman types well or a man tunes an engine with adeptness, it will not be presumed this is all she or he can do. For this reason, all students should receive a broad liberal arts training as long as possible rather than be shunted into specializations too early in life.

- All work will be valued. The laborer, the file clerk, the sales-person, the farm worker will all be esteemed for their con-tribution to the well-being of society.
- Workers will control their activities. Managers will seek and welcome their advice on procedures and policies. Manage-ment's role will be to provide general goals for the work group and to facilitate production needs as the workers de-fine them, not to control worker's lives.
- Work will not be structured around concrete jobs to be filled by individuals. For much work, when a project needs to be done, teams of workers will be assigned to the task. Instead of rewarding the head of a project, all members of a team will accrue benefits equally. (To provide variety, some jobs may allow independent, individual competition, but workers will not earn more by choosing to do these tasks.)
- Tasks need not be filled by full-time workers leaving and ar-riving at the same time. The concepts of "job sharing" and "flex-time" particularly assist women and men who wish to both work and meet family commitments.
- Decision makers will represent and reflect the people whose lives they control. Equal opportunity is necessary in policy-making jobs to ensure all segments of the population have their say in the way businesses, factories, hospitals, schools, and other work places operate. There can be no genuine de-mocracy in America until this representation pervades all institutions.

This ideal tempers the destructive consequences of excess individualism, competition, and hierarchy. Individualism retains its value in that people are urged to explore their talents and contributions to society; however, through team work they can apply these efforts to larger goals than self-aggrandizement. Competition remains, but the rules of the game no longer pit one person explicitly against another. Hierarchies continue, because systems of authority and expertise call for some distribution of responsibility, though teams, often temporary in nature, will hold accountability in many instances. Because the structures for mobility will not be military in model, and the reward structure more compressed and equal than that of today, individuals will not compete for promotion in the usual sense of the word. Work for pay or a false sense of superiority can be supplanted by work for the good of the task and other true reasons—producing a quality product, offering careful service, healing, educating, or whatever.

While the focus here has been upon work restructuring, I do not deny the role of other well-noted factors in economic inequality. One must wonder just how multinational corporate desires secure the perpetuation of the reserve labor force. Certainly the centuries-old system of patriarchy, which eases the private lives of men through the free labor of women, undercuts efforts to obtain basic human rights for our largest disadvantaged group. The pernicious divisive influences of racism pervade social activists as well as conservatives. The histories of other societies, however, document that the people united can defeat such powerful or deeply-ingrained forces.

Starting Young

The most long-reaching changes begin with our children. If they are inculcated with values supportive of social welfare and cooperation, then they will readily create humane institutions that we, beset by competitive drives, can scarcely imagine, let alone implement. The issue here boggles comprehension, as it means changes in family relations, parenting, education, juvenile justice, government, voluntary organizations, and media, and their interactions with one another—all the elements that produce a culture of childhood responsible for directing and shaping youngsters of various backgrounds and appearances into the "right" roles.

The syndicated columnist "Dear Abby" once advised some sixth-graders that maturity is "the ability to do a job whether you're supervised or not; finish a job once it's started . . . and last but not least, the ability to bear injustice without wanting to get even." In other words, become docile, conforming workers who won't cause a stir if they see something wrong. If labor is meaningful, then these behaviors should follow as a matter of course. Rather than use its resources to shape societal roles as spiritually and materially rewarding systems of activity, our society ineffectively and at great expense represses and restricts human potential. As compensation, it allows us the freedom in our leisure time to do what we want or buy what we want (as prompted by advertising), though many of us are too tired or too poor to take advantage of this token liberty.

The details of this suppression process have been documented elsewhere, yet even without statistics the facts are evident to all. Our schools operate under a competitive, individualistic rule book that rewards the exceptional and ignores the wisdom latent in the masses. Kiddy leisure is institutionalized into adult-run organizations, whether ballet school, Boy Scouts, or local soccer league. For every television show like Mister Rogers with its display of sharing, emotional expressiveness, and human respect, there are ten Superheroes hours with their dramatization of aggression, coolness, and flimsy stereotyping. When a child has difficulties, he or she is identified as the source of the problem, and appropriately spanked, drugged, or incarcerated, a foretaste of the blame-the-victim modality applied in adulthood.

Any changes are slow to appear and ambiguous in nature. The Black Freedom schools have disappeared, while the feminists now raise their daughters to be accountants or lawyers. The faces of minority-group members now grace the pages of textbooks, but the teachers who head the classrooms are untutored in ethnic or racial culture. Girls can join athletic teams and be just as driven as their brothers; boys are not urged to cry when it feels appropriate.

Parents whose children are disadvantaged unwittingly foil their best intentions by presuming that the problem is totally within their control. The problem of racism is not blacks, but whites; of sexism, not women, but men; of class bias, not poverty, but privilege. The source is with the people who have resources and power, and who impose their values and social order upon those who don't. Yet the focus of much "new" socialization is to turn disadvantaged youngsters into copies of privileged ones—for example, to make girls into boys. The result is still a facsimile, and without the genuine quality of maleness, the penis, the imitation can only fail. The sad outcome for the culture as a whole is an increasing restriction on those personal traits and qualities considered healthy in mature adults—those male-identified characteristics that have served so many destructive forces in our society.

Because the people at the top venerate competition, the winning element, they fail to understand that the inclusion of variety contributes to the society as a whole. When men are raised to be insecure and defensive, they perceive anyone different to be a foe, rather than a representative of another slice of reality, one complementary to theirs. They miss the point that all could gain by multiple vision. Individualism, competition, and conflict are not in themselves villains to be thrown out of our culture; the problem rests in the fact that these values are the sole driving motive for most social action, both at work and in love.

A radical socialization policy would explore ways in which to balance the polar value systems that shape our society, and in so doing, give our citizens a rich repertoire of choices for constructing their world. Those who want to change the culture of childhood must move beyond the facile solutions (which are often those that seem manageable within their slim resources) toward activities that cut into the deep fabric of our culture and piece in alternative manners of perceiving, evaluating, and acting. This takes vision, audacity, courage, and the willingness to make a lot of mistakes. The critique is an old one; it is time for action.

Challenging the Gatekeepers

The role of unions as an immediate positive force in decreasing inequality cannot be underestimated. On the one hand, they have in recent years given way to reactionary demands and become associations protective of the interests of some workers. Those without benefit of their clout have grown impatient as they pay higher prices to provide services and benefits to union people, and watch their own paychecks shrink in actual value. On the other hand, the demands of unions do affect the wages of nonunion workers. For all the problems large unions have encountered in recent years—demagogic leadership, corruption by organized crime, brutality toward competing labor organizations—they continue to be a critical power base that succeeds in securing certain benefits that workers would otherwise be unlikely to get.

In growing into ponderous, insular bureaucracies, unions have lost the vitality of the late thirties, a time when the desire to bring all workers into the fold was of primary concern. Seventy percent of the workers in this country are sitting ripe for organization, yet no one moves toward them. If a union wanted to wield extraordinary power, it would only need to enlist the secretaries and clerks who keep the machines of large corporations operating. Yet clerical workers remain the largest nonunionized work force today.

Union leaders worrying about the deterioration of membership can revitalize interest by introducing new demands, ones that move beyond protectionism to job design and control. Insistence on rigid job ladders and seniority rights has left workers well-paid and bored. That "job enrichment" and "worker democracy" techniques are being introduced to some work places at the insistence of management—not organized labor—reflects the outmoded and out-of-touch mental set of current labor leadership.

Actually, given the deterioration of unions, it is promising that so many workers remain unorganized, for they can now join together free of the deleterious customs of established labor groups. An organization of clerical workers could develop leadership from its own body, predominantly women, who would know how to run the group in ways that would meet the needs of working women. Labor unity would thus give lower-level workers a feeling of efficacy, self-esteem, and social worth they are unable to find on the job.

Yet new worker organizations would be no panacea. They might imitate their older brothers and emphasize narrow, protective demands such as seniority rights and control over hiring, firing, and layoff, rather than address the broader social needs of workers such as safe working conditions, job sharing, flexible work-plans, parental-care leaves, and innovations in work organization. Certainly established unions would try to move in as soon as any sign of successful unity emerged. The bone-deep issues of racism and sexism remain. Would union truck drivers respect the picket line of secretaries?

For the real world in the end of the twentieth century, this opportunity, however conflict-ridden its results, cannot be allowed to pass. The voices and sacrifices of early unionists must be given heed, and the organization of all workers move forward.

Unlike unions, which have had a rich, if inconsistent record of social concern, professional organizations have existed for the explicit monopoly over knowledge and activity in society. It is amazing to consider that since the emergence of humanity, women throughout much of the world have given birth, and continue to do so, assisted only by one another, unencumbered by "experts." But in "civilized" countries such as the United States, birthing has become a mysterious, trouble-laden event to be controlled by doctors. In little more than one century's time, a small group of people have uprooted one of the most meaningful rituals in a family's life and thrust it into a strange setting, beyond the control of the parents. Similarly, disagreements between neighbors become a matter not of direct confrontation but of the lawyers and the courts. Knowledge is now valid only if it comes from the mouths of academics, preferably those at Harvard or other elite schools.

Assuredly there is nothing inherently wrong with expert groups forming together. Medicine is a healing system that in the case of certain disorders is superior to folk care—and vice versa. The difficulty is that as social institutions, medicine, law, academia, and other professions have acted with scarce concern for the public. They have become societal nobles, practicing noblesse oblige, which, as everyone knows, is doing things for the nobles while saying the changes are for the people. As with other institutions in society, the professions have suffered from the loss of collective interest and public morality. They all have their code of ethics, but they seem to invoke them seriously only when under attack. Drunken doctors perform operations, lawyers practice conflict of interest, and college professors use their grading power to seduce undergraduate men and women. As individuals, professionals are as venal as the rest of us—this is why their organizations are supposed to guarantee that we will not be taken in by inept, incompetent, or salacious practitioners. It is in trade for this promise of competence that we have granted them the mandate to control their own activities.

Having been a member of professional organizations for over fifteen years, ones composed of people supposedly interested in social welfare, I see little hope of expecting these bodies to be born again, recant, and welcome minorities and women into their arms as colleagues. The privileged white men in these groups, the best and the brightest, simply don't want their private clubs disturbed. They don't want their lives complicated by people who look and act different, whose experiences lead to other ways of looking at the world than the conventional ones. They can't face the fact that the world is bursting with others of considerable talent or insight, that they are not the chosen few blessed by God with unique gifts. They want to be special, not just one part of humanity.

Consequently, the most viable attack upon the professions must be from the outside. One efficacious, though slow attack would be on training. First, we could see that sons and daughters from families unlikely to send children into the professions get them there, whether through personal encouragement, financial aid, or wise academic counseling. Second, we can become cantankerous and demanding clients of the professions, forcing them to face a dialogue with us or else face the threat of losing their secure autonomy. This means resisting their counterclaims that women, minorities, and others will lower the quality of the profession. It is likely that as women and blacks move into medicine, doctors will not be able to charge as much—but the medical care will certainly not be any worse, and in some ways, we can expect that the entry of people with different cultural backgrounds will only breathe life into more rigid areas of practice. Finally, we must insist that the federal government make several firm prosecutions of professional schools, organizations, and related groups that practice blatant discrimination. Were Harvard or Berkeley slapped with the federal bias suits they deserve, our women and poorer people would suddenly find many role models in front of the classrooms.

Bolstering Small Business's Role

The most difficult arena demanding change is that affecting workers in the market and monopoly economies. Workers in free-enterprise firms should not be penalized because their employers chose to be independent owners, or because they work in fields the corporations find too risky to absorb. If anything, workers in risky or competitive firms should get higher wages than their corporate kin, since they are more prone to seasonal, part-time, or temporary work. If construction workers earn large hourly wages for this reason, then so should garment workers, canners, resort workers, and others. As we have seen, budgets in these companies and services have little slack to allow for liberal pay and benefits.

What is needed, then, is a nationwide commitment to the notion that every worker deserves a fair and adequate wage. Since the economy has not designed work in a way that everyone can get a good, forty-hour-week job, then those who must fill the less steady jobs, whether for interest, geographic location, or whatever, deserve a liveable income. The solution must be a federal one. One possibility is a wage subsidy to market firms to ensure that employees earn not only a basic wage, but receive medical, retirement, and other benefits as well. This proposal may seem unduly radical to some, for its largesse and giving away money, and reactionary to others, for its willingness to pad the pockets of employers, however temporarily. It is neither.

The country has already established systems whereby both people without work and large corporations can get survival funds. If we are willing to save the workers of Lockheed and Chrysler, then why not make life better for those of Ace Hat Factory or Johnny's Dry Cleaning? It is the people in these latter firms who are being squeezed, for they are neither eligible for nor desire welfare, yet they do not get the perquisites of their cousins in large companies. In effect, monies now going to social service agencies would transfer to people through the market economy. In time, the gains would outstrip early costs.

What is needed is more than financial encouragement of equal opportunity in small business; the government must also simplify its regulatory approach. A solution here would be to amend the Civil Rights Act exemption of businesses with less than 15 employees to include those with less than 100. This change would capture the bulk of market firms in many localities. In place of the elaborate data-collection and detailed program plans currently required by law would be procedures more appropriate for small firms. If the EEOC had numerous field offices, then specialists acquainted with the typical local businesses could develop realistic and efficient procedures and timetables for owners. Complementing this ideosyncratic implementation of regulations would be an arbitration department to which employees in a lawyer's office, small plastics plant, or health club could take equal-opportunity complaints for resolution.

A Case Illustration

While speculating on ways to reduce inequality that would reject the premises of the American Dream, I asked myself what the largest group of disadvantaged workers were and the clearest ways they could be helped. That group is office help.

These people, mostly women, have most likely gotten their

training by taking the business curriculum in high school. My first recommendation would be to eliminate this option completely. Instead, all students would take a liberal arts program, for it is this broad curriculum of theory, practice, and values that helps young adults to develop the ability to make wise choices in any area of life, particularly for a society where technology is constantly changing the daily features of work. By going through this curriculum, too, young women will have a better range of experiences from which to select a career. As it is now, girls without interest in college at age thirteen sign up for the business track without thought. Thirteen is a very young age to make a decision with lifelong implications.

Eliminating the business curriculum makes good political sense as well. In these times of decreasing educational budgets, we must ask why public schools should provide the job training for firms with offices. Secretarial training should be put in the hands of those who benefit from it—the employers. Were this the case, then employers would be faced with two problems: the additional expense of on-the-job training and that of providing sufficient rewards to keep trained employees with the firm. The result would be an increase in work quality and financial reward for clerical help. The other possibility would be that students go to secretarial schools after high school, in which case they will want to demand more from employers for the investment they have made in themselves. (The schoolteachers who currently teach in public schools could only gain by moving into the private sector, where they can count upon better earnings and rewards.)

This illustration leads neatly into another proposal, one that concerns affirmative-action hiring. The emphasis in this area has been to see that employers are placing women and minorities in jobs once reserved for privileged white men. But the problem with the segregated labor markets is that predominantly minority or female jobs are tainted and earn fewer dollars. Thus, a wise implementation of affirmative action would require that employers place white men in these preserves. If office help were reflective of the general working population, half of the secretaries would be male. These men would not likely be asked to darn socks and buy a present for the boss' wife; if they aren't asked to do so, then the women can't be either.

For the smoothest changeover, the introduction of men into female work cannot be done bit by bit, just as women can't be placed as lone tokens in management. The sole male in the typing force would be taken as odd or unusual by male bosses (or as a candidate for quick promotion). Also, women colleagues would find the appearance of one male stenographer more disturbing than that of five.

One way to assist this solution would be to make clerical work the first and necessary entry level for managerial work. This makes excellent sense for training purposes. Clerical workers have access to information many administrators miss. In addition to dealing with client complaints and needs on a day-to-day basis, processing forms, and reading every type of communication produced by the firm, secretaries hear and see informal actions on many levels of the organization. Furthermore, clerical activity offers a reasonable simulation for managerial skills, for it requires the ability to plan and structure activity, to respond to many different demands under pressure, to act decisively, and to behave with tact toward others. (The skills themselves are valuable to the manager working at home, on the road, or in the office alone after hours.)

Next, clerical jobs would be reevaluated and paid accordingly, so men would be only delighted to move into these positions. Consider an industry like life insurance, where agents (predominantly men) earn about seven times as much as secretaries, who, according to one analysis, do about two-thirds of the agents' work.[1] Companies might respond by rigging the job titles and evaluations to keep agents privileged. But a smart management would gradually cut back and redefine the agent's role, making secretaries and agents variations on the same job, that of insurance salesperson, with more equal pay for all (and fewer high salaries to a few). This would also open the way for sales teams to replace the individual competition, more a disadvantage than companies may realize, with creative cooperative sales approaches.

Many of these suggestions do not touch the plight of women in small offices all over the country. Here the government should provide some incentive, perhaps a tax break, to small-business owners who demonstrate they are paying clerical help at more than marginal wages. The Department of Labor could establish yearly profiles for fair secretarial pay in various regions of the country as a basis for this decision. Second, clerical workers in these firms must have access to an ombudsperson to arbitrate cases of unfair treatment, sexual harassment, and related grievances.

THE PROMISE

Christopher Lasch has painted the United States as a culture of narcissism, where people turn inward on themselves, increase the distances from others, in an attempt to make sense of a chaotic and exploitative world.[2] Their solution only exacerbates the problem, because the more each soul keeps to its own dialogue, the less likely the wisdom borne of collective thought can proffer the cure. We return home from dangerous, empty, or boring jobs embittered and beset against ourselves. To compensate, we release our frustrations on our families and express a vacuous self-esteem through consumption of trivial goods of poor quality. The inflation of individualism pushes success away from our grasp—something is always wrong with ourselves, and if we do manage to pull together the right image, fad and fashion will ridicule it a year or two later.

Lasch captures only one side of our Janus-headed culture. It is not that what he says is wrong so much as it is incomplete. He misses sight of countervailing forces of another strand in American culture that keeps the society from dying an entropic collapse. The underside of American life is the spirit of community and sharing, obvious in the extraordinary web of voluntary activities in any neighborhood. It is in the bonding of unrelated people across households into friendship groups that form fictive families. It is in the tenacity of blood ties across thousands of miles of physical separation.

These activities go unnoticed for several reasons. For one, they represent one of the few places in life where people can meet together and choose their own destinies and interdependencies. Since there is no tax profit in the results, the government keeps no accounts or regulations. Because little direct material gain accrues to individuals, the measure of reward must come from an internal judge, one who calculates on ethical and moral grounds, not financial ones. Academics and social critics, ensconced in individualistic and emotionally repressive settings, mock and ridicule the public response to some dramatic news story tragedy as maudlin or superficial. It is not the mawkishness of charity telethons that makes them bizarre—it is the irony that millions of people are desperate to share with others and lack a way of making personal contact.

All strands of contemporary social criticism, from conservative through liberal to radical, dehumanize the public by ultimately throwing blame upon them for their troubles. The conservatives want people to work harder. The liberals, in refusing to nail any one in particular, leave us feeling inadequate and ultimately to blame for ourselves. The radicals are not afraid to indict the economic and political elite of the nation for its ills, but in practice they fight among themselves and attack one another for not going about the revolution in the politically correct way. The dignity, good will, and strength of people are ignored in the debates. Meanwhile the public goes about its lives, wisely mistrustful of all sides that, by their actions, show a basic contempt for average, anonymous workers.

When asked to rank values that are most important for a good life, Americans will place at the top of the list health, a good marriage, good family life, and a good country to live in.[3] A large bank account comes out last. When asked to select the most important characteristic of a good job, we will say "meaning," and place pay and benefits far down the list. When asked how we would like to see federal monies budgeted, we want less spent on foreign aid, space, and welfare, and more on health care, drug addiction, crime prevention, environmental protection, big city problems, and education.

The surface display of American society disguises these deep-felt desires for community and intimacy. The consumer economy tempts us away from putting people before property and products. We dutifully eat chemically-laden foods, wear plastic clothes, ride in unsafe vehicles, and use dangerous drugs because we have little other choice in our busy, machine-ruled lifestyle. In spite of our desire for more expenditures in the area of human services, our government's largest budget expense is for military and defense. Since bombs, bombers, and soldiers are less visible than poor welfare mothers, we slash at the wrong budget items when taxes pinch our purses.

If we are willing to bear the schizophrenia of the times, wanting more love while buying more objects, marching through the days without protesting our war-based economy, it is because in many areas of value our lives are full. The majority of us report pleasure over the state of our health, marriage, and family life. Perhaps because we do feel thanks for these bounties, we bear the deadening trials of the job. Surveys on quality of work life in recent years show a steady decline in satisfaction, notably in the areas of health and safety (which concern eight out of ten workers), inadequate fringe benefits, unpleasant physical conditions, transportation problems, and inconvenient or excessive hours. Few of us find on the job the meaning we long for.[4]

Out of a condition of work dissatisfaction, coalitions can be forged among previously distant or conflicting groups. Disadvantaged workers—women, blacks, people with disabilities— have higher rates of displeasure than white men, but many of the latter are unhappy for similar reasons. These dissatisfactions share common roots, growing out of the narrow, inequitable, competitive, segregating work structures of our society. So long as women are excluded from physical work, men will labor under dangerous and health-destroying conditions. So long as blacks sit at the bottom of the corporate ladder, white men from eastern and southern European backgrounds will perch just as immobile a rung or two above. So long as companies can move to take advantage of a cheap suburban female labor force, men working in these areas will earn below parity as well. Though most are blind to these facts, the average white male workers share some conditions with those of the disadvantaged. However, privileged males see that these men receive just enough extra gains to bolster a false sense of security and superiority.

Though any major change will require that disadvantaged groups overcome their competitiveness and recognize their shared economic fates, genuinely revolutionary changes in work structures must incorporate those white males who are implicated in the process of subordination. The simplest appeal would be through personal ties. Just as union men once redefined their views of women when they observed the cunning and bravery of their wives, mothers, and sisters during strikes, so, too, working men today can be shown the facts of women's labor and its degradation. They can see how their financial struggles are tied directly to the underpayment of the female wage earner. (Unfortunately, no analogous personal connection can be drawn for an understanding between races.)

Collective demands for a new work life can only benefit the quality of life in the society as a whole. At a time of diminishing energy reserves, widespread pollution, faltering health care, increasing functional illiteracy, inflation, and declining trust in government, the nation must encourage the full use of citizens' talents and abilities. More than ever, workers should be directed to create, innovate, and cooperate in halting the catastrophic course we seem to have chosen. The crisis in work productivity that underlies our current economic instability is a crisis in spirit, a warning from workers that the policy makers and employers can no longer afford to ignore.

Were American culture as narcissistic as Christopher Lasch has claimed, the efforts of those of us committed to "liberty and justice for all" would be in vain. Were all white men satisfied with their work, the labor market would be too ossified to hope of change. The conditions for a new order are present. We need only to be delivered of our delusionary dreams to see the promise in the reality about us.

Notes

Chapter One

1. John Saffin, *A Brief and Candid Answer to a Late Printed Sheet Entitled The Selling of Joseph* (Boston, 1700), as quoted in Stephen Foster, *Their Solitary Way* (New Haven: Yale University Press, 1971), p. 15.

2. Thomas Hooker, *A Survey of the Summe of Church Doctrine,* (Boston, 1648), as quoted in Foster, p. 14.

3. William Perkins, *A Treatise of the Callings of Men* (Cambridge, 1604), as quoted in Foster, p. 102.

4. Source ambiguous. See quote and fn. 74 in Foster, p. 123.

5. This is elaborated in Foster. See also Jackson Turner Main, *The Social Structure of Revolutionary America* (Princeton: Princeton University Press, 1965).

6. Main, *Social Structure;* and Gary B. Nash, ed., *Class and Society in America* (Englewood Cliffs: Prentice-Hall, 1970).

7. Not all historians accept the thesis argued here, as Nash's introductory essay, "Social Structure and the Interpretation of Colonial American History," makes evident. I am inclined to support this view, since it is consistent with sociological studies of community uprisings, particularly those that point to "relative deprivation" as a basis for change.

8. "Eumenes," *N.J. Journal,* May 10, 1780, as quoted in Main, p. 236.

9. Historians have long seen Franklin as a symbol for the shift from Puritanism toward a modern image of achievement. Some of these essays may be found in David Levin, ed., *The Puritan in the Enlightenment: Franklin and Edwards* (Chicago: Rand McNally, 1963); Charles L. Safford, ed., *Benjamin Franklin and the American Character* (Boston: Heath, 1955).

10. The role of social factors in Franklin's rise is best illustrated in David Freeman Hawke, *Franklin* (New York: Harper and Row, 1976).

11. Noah Webster, Jr., Esq., *Effects of Slavery on Morals and Industry*, as quoted in J. R. Pole, *The Pursuit of Equality in American History* (Berkeley: University of California, 1978), p. 118.

12. Two useful summary sources for the inspirational literature discussed in this section are Richard Weiss, *The American Myth of Success* (New York: Basic Books, 1969), and Irvin G. Wyllie, *The Self-Made Man in America* (New York: Free Press, 1954).

13. Orison S. Marden, *The Young Man Entering Business* (New York, 1903), p. 27. Marden was editor of *Success* magazine.

14. William Holmes McGuffey, *McGuffey's Newly Revised Eclectic Third Reader* (Cincinnati, 1843), as quoted in Wyllie, *Self-Made Man*, p. 33.

15. Alger's stories are more moralistic than contemporary beliefs about them realize. Naked acquisitiveness is never the goal.

16. Kenneth S. Lynn, *The Dream of Success* (Boston: Little, Brown, 1955), discusses the impact of the myth on these and other novelists. Though Jack London criticized the myth in his best writing, such as *Martin Eden*, he clung to it as the basis for his personal life.

17. In *Will to Believe and Other Essays* (New York: Longmans, Green, 1910) William James proposed that "faith in a fact can help create the fact," and thus that an individual could regulate his or her own life.

18. This summary is based upon my examination of the 1900 and 1910 U.S. Census reports.

19. Erhard's doctrines are much at home with the New Thought devotees of the turn of the century; both place central emphasis upon the purported ability of individuals to design their own lives and change "reality" to accommodate their needs.

20. See, for example, Richard Bolles, *The Three Boxes of Life* (Berkeley: Ten Speed Press, 1978). My comments are not meant to attack the entirety of the approaches suggested by Erhard, Bolles, and others, so much as to indicate faults in the basic premises of their theories, and to point out that their ideas are hardly novel, but spring up repeatedly in U.S. cultural history.

21. Richard P. Coleman and Lee Rainwater, *Social Standing in America* (New York: Basic Books, 1978).

Chapter Two

1. Primary sources for discussion of Allan Bakke's life are the *New York Times* and *Washington Post* of June 28 and 29, 1978. A thoughtful history of the Bakke case, one which appeared after the drafting of this chapter, is Allan P. Sindler, *Bakke, DeFunis, and Minority Admissions* (New York: Longmans, 1978).

2. This material on comparative medical school competition is dis-

cussed in several of the Bakke briefs. See especially the *Amicus* brief, U.S. Supreme Court, *Bakke*, Association of American Medical Colleges.

3. See data in *Amicus* brief, U.S. Supreme Court, *Bakke*, Rutgers–The State University, as well as Charles E. Odegaard, *Minorities in Medicine* (New York: The Josiah Macy, Jr. Foundation, 1977).

4. Details on the Davis medical school applications are in *Amicus* brief, University of California, U.S. Supreme Court, *Bakke*.

5. Petition of the University of California, U.S. Supreme Court, *Bakke*.

6. The *Amicus* brief, U.S. Supreme Court, *Bakke*, Law School Admissions Council, provides an excellent defense for these arguments.

7. For details see the respective *Amicus* brief, U.S. Supreme Court, *Bakke*, Black Law Student Association at University of California-Berkeley, and the NAACP Defense and Education Fund.

8. Bakke wrote Peter Storandt on August 7, 1973: "My first concern is to be allowed to study medicine, and—challenging the concept of racial quotas is secondary." The full text is in the Trial Record, California Supreme Court, *Bakke*.

9. Storandt's letters appear in *Amicus* brief, U.S. Supreme Court, *Bakke*, National Organization for Women, and others. See also Sindler, *Bakke, Defunis, and Minority Admissions*, pp. 69–73.

10. Sindler, p. 65.

11. Sindler, p. 81.

12. I had the fortune of reading the Bakke briefs in the weeks just preceding the Supreme Court decision. I quickly concluded that Bakke's lawyers had done a masterful job, as their skill and persuasive ability convinced me, one ideologically opposed to his position at the time, of his claim. The split decision finally reached by the justices appeared the only reasonable solution given the evidence. See also Charles Lawrence II, "The Bakke Case," *Saturday Review*, October 15, 1977.

13. This fact was revealed in the Los Angeles *Times*, July 5, 1976, and July 14, 1976. Davis later revised this policy. This important fact was neglected by most analyses of the case appearing in news media and magazines prior to and following the court decision.

14. *Amicus* brief, U.S. Supreme Court, *Bakke*, Committee on Academic Non-discrimination and Integrity.

15. *Amicus* brief, U.S. Supreme Court, *Bakke*, American Federation of Teachers.

Chapter Three

1. New York *Times,* February 28, 1978.

2. Opinion, Justice Thurgood Marshall, U.S. Supreme Court, *Bakke.*

3. Norman Bradburn, *The Structure of Psychological Well-Being* (Chicago: Aldine, 1969).

4. Reynolds Farley, "Trends in Racial Inequalities: Have the Gains of the 1960s Disappeared in the 1970s?" *American Sociological Review* 42 (1977): 189–208. Farley says the gains have remained, though an inspection of his data may lead to other conclusions.

5. For example, Karen Mason, John L. Czajka, and Sara Arber, "Change in U.S. Women's Sex Role Attitudes," *American Sociological Review* 41 (1976): 573–596.

6. Conclusions discussed in subsequent sections are based upon my own examination of yearly economic indicators from 1950 to the present. My initial draft of this chapter was cumbersome with the details of that work. After the manuscript was completed, I discovered a 1978 publication by the U.S. Commission on Civil Rights, *Social Indicators of Equality for Minorities and Women.* This volume, based upon a more sophisticated analysis of the data I studied, provided the basis for a redraft of this chapter. Anyone who doubts my conclusions is advised to look at this volume, or graph out the statistics published in the *Monthly Labor Report* and relevant Census agency documents.

7. Contrary to what many believe, black men have not always had lower work force experience than whites. Between 1910 and 1930, they actually had a higher participation rate. For example, in 1910, 87 percent of black males over 10 years of age were gainfully employed, in contrast with 79 percent of white males. In light of this evidence, it is clear that black men's economic situation with regard to participation has decreased. For further discussion of this point, see Edna Bonacich, "Advanced Capitalism and Black/White Relations in the United States," *American Sociological Review* 41 (1976): 34–51.

8. Robert N. Stern, Walter R. Gove, and Omer R. Galle, "Equality for Blacks and Women: An Essay on Relative Progress," *Social Science Quarterly* 56 (1976): 664–672. These figures are for 1970 data. The writers' statistical analyses verify my descriptive one here, in that their indices show how women are not experiencing acceptance in many jobs, while blacks are finding a few more doors open to them now than in the past.

9. For a discussion of occupational prestige scores, see Lloyd V. Temme, *Occupation: Meanings and Measures* (Washington, D.C.: Bureau of Social Science Research, 1975).

10. The Bureau of Labor Statistics publishes its unemployment findings in the monthly report *Employment and Earnings*. An unusually concise presentation of the data collection and problems in interpretation of unemployment rates is Alan L. Sorkin, *Education, Unemployment, and Economic Growth* (Lexington, Mass.: D. C. Heath, 1975).

11. John C. Leggett and Jerry Gioglio, *Breaking Out of the Double Digit* (New Brunswick, N.J.: New Brunswick Cooperative Press, 1977).

12. Carol J. Loomis, "AT&T in the Throes of Equal Employment," *Fortune* (January 15, 1979): 45–57.

13. Sally L. Hacker, "Sex Stratification, Technology, and Organizational Change," *Social Problems* 26 (1979): 539–557.

14. *Amicus* brief, U.S. Supreme Court, *Bakke*, National Polish Congress and others.

15. Two important exceptions to the general neglect of the economic disadvantages of minority groups other than women and blacks are Vernon Briggs, Jr., Walter Fogel, and Fred H. Schmidt, *The Chicano Worker* (Austin: University of Texas, 1977), and Betty Lee Sung, *A Survey of Chinese-American Manpower and Employment* (New York: Praeger, 1976).

Chapter Four

1. My indebtedness to the work of Winthrop D. Jordan, *White Over Black* (Chapel Hill: University of North Carolina, 1968) throughout this section is major. Also influential were the writings of John L. Hodge, Donald K. Struckman, and Lynn Dorland Trost, *Cultural Bases of Racism and Oppression* (Berkeley: Two Riders Press, 1975).

2. Jordan, *White over Black*, p. 4. The writer is M. John Hawkins, an English voyager who published his observations in 1598.

3. Thomas Jefferson, *Notes on the State of Virginia* (Chapel Hill: University of North Carolina, 1955).

4. White's book, *An Account of the Regular Gradation in Man, and in Different Animals and Vegetables; and from The Former to the Latter* is discussed in Jordan, p. 499f.

5. Racism pervaded all of Spencer's writings; the most popular of his works was his *Principles of Sociology*, published in two parts in 1894 and 1896.

6. Edward Alsworth Ross, a major figure in early American sociology, was never described as a racist when I was taking theory courses in graduate school in the early 1960s. The truth came to light one day when I was presiding over the E. A. Ross Club, the sociology graduate club at the University of Wisconsin. A fellow student asked that we change the name of the organization, and proceeded to read some of Ross' blatant anti-Semitism. The club decided to defer the decision

because we learned that Ross's wife was still alive and living in the area. This quote comes from his study of *The Old World in the New*, (New York: Century, 1914).

7. Theodore Roosevelt, *The Winning of the West*, 1 (New York: Scribner's, 1926).

8. Although at the turn of the century a few suffragists believed in women's equality to men in all regards, the large majority preferred ideas such as those of Charlotte Perkins Gilman, who emphasized that women had special values to bring to society, particularly in the areas of humanistic concern, such as childrearing and inducing a spirit of cooperation among diverse peoples. A good introduction to the changing role of women in U.S. history is Mary P. Ryan, *Womanhood in America* (New York: New Viewpoints, 1975).

9. For references to stereotype research, see Nancy G. Kutner, "Use of an Updated Adjective Check-List in Research on Ethnic Stereotypes," *Social Science Quarterly* 54 (1973): 639–645.

10. Arthur Jensen, *Genetics and Education* (New York: Harper and Row, 1972). Shockley relied upon the work of psychologist Cyril Burt, whose studies we now know to be fraudulent.

11. For a detailed presentation of this argument, see Clarice Stasz Stoll, *Female and Male* (Dubuque, Iowa: Wm. C. Brown, 1978), chap. 3.

12. Steven Goldberg, *The Inevitability of Patriarchy* (London: Temple Smith, 1977).

13. For example, Janet Shibley Hyde and B. G. Rosenberg, *Half the Human Experience* (Lexington: D. C. Heath, 1976), pp. 260–269.

14. For more detail, see Stoll, *Female and Male*, chap. 5.

15. Jan J. Durkin, "The Potential of Women," in Bette Ann Stead, *Women in Management* (Englewood Cliffs, N.J.: Prentice-Hall, 1978).

Chapter Five

1. Joe R. Feagan, "Poverty: We Still Believe That God Helps Those Who Help Themselves," *Psychology Today* 6 (1972): 101ff.

2. Joan Huber and William H. Form, *Income and Ideology* (New York: Free Press, 1973).

3. For example, Robert V. Robinson and Wendell Bell, "Equality, Success and Social Justice in England and the United States," *American Sociological Review* 43 (1978): 125–143.

4. Edward Banfield, *The Unheavenly City* (Boston: Little, Brown, 1976).

5. Nathan Glazer and Daniel P. Moynihan, *Beyond the Melting Pot* (Cambridge, Mass.: MIT Press, 1963), p. 64.

6. For example, Gary Becker, "Investment in Human Capital,"

Journal of Political Economy, Supplement (1962): 9–49; also his *Human Capital* (New York: National Bureau of Economic Research, 1975).

7. Lester Thurow, *Investment in Human Capital* (Belmont: Wadsworth, 1970), p. 89.

8. This argument is not limited to neoconservatives. See, for example, Raymond S. Franklin and Solomon Resnick, *The Political Economy of Racism* (New York: Holt, Rinehart, & Winston, 1973), p. 48f.

9. The major proponents of this view are Jacob Mincer and Solomon Polachek, e.g., "Family Investments in Human Capital: Earnings of Women," *Journal of Political Economy* 82 (1974): S76–S108.

10. Alan Sorkin, *Education, Unemployment, and Economic Growth* (Lexington, Mass.: D. C. Heath, 1974).

11. A simple check on this data is through census reports. See also Sorkin (1974) and Lester Thurow, *Poverty and Discrimination* (Washington, D.C.: The Brookings Institution, 1969).

12. The classic study on the female work force since 1900 is Valerie K. Oppenheimer, *The Female Labor Force in the United States* (Berkeley: Institute of International Studies, 1970). On working wives, see Linda J. Waite, "Working Wives: 1940–1960," *American Sociological Review* 40 (1975): 174–200.

13. Mincer and Polachek, "Family Investment." As sociologist Otis Dudley Duncan observed in a "Comment" on Mincer's work, the sample size was tiny and measurements crude, and the authors "seemingly read their tables a little too smoothly." *Journal of Political Economy* 82 (1974): S109–S110.

14. For a check, refer to the Department of Labor's *Employment and Earnings.*

15. For critical reviews of these studies, see James Kirkpatrick, "Testing and Fair Employment," in Kent Miller and Ralph Mason Dreeger, *Comparative Studies of Blacks and Whites in the U.S.* (New York: Academic Press, 1975); Judith Long Laws, "Psychological Dimensions of Labor Force Participation of Women," in Phyllis A. Wallace, *Employment Opportunity and the AT&T Case* (Cambridge, Mass.: MIT Press, 1976); Judith Long Laws, "Work Aspiration of Women," in Martha Blaxall and Barbara Reagan, *Women and the Workplace* (Chicago: University of Chicago, 1976).

16. Again, these conclusions may be verified by examining census reports and Department of Labor statistics that display the occupations held by persons at various educational levels.

17. In sociology, this is one of the most popular—and prestigious—areas of study, often misnamed "social stratification," the process of class formation, when it is actually a narrow concern with individual achievement. Many papers of this type can be found in

issues of the *American Sociological Review* between 1955 and 1975. For a collection of papers in this tradition, see William H. Sewell, Robert Hauser, and David L. Featherman, *Schooling and Achievement in American Society* (New York: Academic Press, 1976).

18. All studies of the effects of human capital variables mentioned here employ techniques whereby other sources of discrimination are controlled for or held constant. This reference is to David L. Featherman and Robert Hauser, "Sexual Inequalities and Socioeconomic Achievement in the U.S.: 1962–1973," *American Sociological Review* 41 (1976): 189–208.

19. Robert Bibb and William Form, "The Effects of Industrial, Occupational and Sex Stratification on Wages in Blue-collar Workers," *Social Forces* 55 (1977): 974–996.

20. Jerolyn Lyle and Jane L. Ross, *Women in Industry* (Lexington, Mass.: D. C. Heath, 1973). See also Orley Ashenfelter and Albert Rees, *Discrimination in Labor Markets* (Princeton: Princeton University Press, 1972).

21. Stephen Michelson, *Income of Racial Minorities* (Washington, D.C.: The Brookings Institution, 1968). Also see G. Donald Jud and James L. Walker, "How Racial Bias and Social Status Affect the Earnings of Young Men," *Monthly Labor Review* 100, 4 (1977): 44–5; Joan Gustafson Haworth, James Gwartney, and Charles Haworth, "Earnings, Productivity, and Changes in Employment Discrimination," *American Economic Review* 65 (1975): 156–158; Dudley Posten, Jr., and David Alvirez, "On the Cost of Being a Mexican-American Worker," *Social Science Quarterly* 53 (1973): 697–709. Ross M. Stolzenberg, "Education, Occupation, and Wage Differences Between White and Black Men," *American Journal of Sociology* 81 (1975): 299–323.

22. Oris Dudley Duncan, "Inheritance of Poverty or Inheritance of Race?" in Daniel Moynihan, *Understanding Poverty* (New York, 1969).

23. Stanley H. Masters, *Black-White Income Differentials* (New York: Academic Press, 1975).

24. James S. Coleman, *Survey of Equal Educational Opportunity* (Washington, D.C.: U.S. Government Printing Office, 1966).

25. Barbara Bergman, "The Effect on White Incomes of Discrimination in Employment," *Journal of Political Economy* 79 (1971): 294–313.

26. Christopher Jencks, *Who Gets Ahead?* (New York: Basic Books, 1979).

27. This is a small oversimplification. Someone who completes one year of college also benefits. So the student who drops out of college gains little by leaving after the second or third year. He or she should drop out early or finish if maximum achievement payoff is the only goal. See Jencks, *Who Gets Ahead?*, chapter six.

Chapter Six

1. The best recent study of these hopes is Linda Gottfredson, *Race and Sex Differences in Occupational Aspiration*, Report No. 254, Baltimore: Center for Social Organization of Schools, Johns Hopkins University, 1978.

2. Studs Terkel, *Working* (New York: Pantheon, 1974), and Harry Braverman, *Labor and Monopoly Capital* (New York: Monthly Review Press, 1974).

3. A thoughtful, nontechnical review of these problems is found in several articles of *Psychology Today*, September 1979.

4. Leon Kamin, *The Science and Politics of IQ* (New York: Lawrence Erlbaum, 1974).

5. A major analysis of this process is Samuel Bowles and Herbert Gintis, *Schooling in Capitalist America* (New York: Basic Books, 1976). For an opposing view, see Richard A. Rehberg and Evelyn R. Rosenthal, *Class and Merit in the American High School* (New York: Longman, 1978).

6. This thesis has not been fully explored to date. A good position paper is Carol Kehr Tittle, *Sex Bias in Testing*, Women's Educational Equity Communications Network, 1978.

7. For an introduction to the literature in this section, see Henry Jay Becker, *How Young People Find Career Entry Jobs*, Report No. 241, Baltimore: Center for Study of Schools, 1977, as well as his Report No. 281, *Personal Networks of Opportunity in Obtaining Jobs*, 1979.

8. Lester Thurow, *Generating Inequality* (New York: Basic Books, 1975).

9. Richard N. Bolles, *The Three Boxes of Life* (Berkeley: Ten Speed Press, 1978).

10. Becker, *Personal Networks*.

11. This discussion of agencies is based upon Thomas Martinez, *The Human Marketplace* (New Brunswick: Transaction Books, 1976).

12. This research, unpublished, was done by sociologist Carl Jensen, and reported through personal communication.

13. These data are readily available in census reports, which present the percentage female or percentage black for the most common jobs in our society.

14. Harriet Zellner, "Discrimination Against Women, Occupational Segregation, and the Relative Wage," *American Economic Review Proceedings* (1972): 157–166; Stephen D. McLaughlin, "Occupational Sex Identification and the Assessment of Male and Female Earnings Inequality," *American Sociological Review* 43 (1978): 909–921.

15. A good review of the evidence supporting my claims here is Marijane Suelzle, "Women in Labor," *Transaction* 8 (1970): 50–58.

16. Terkel, *Working*; Barbara Garson, *All the Livelong Day* (New York: Penguin, 1977).

17. See Lyn Farley, *Sexual Shakedown* (New York: McGraw-Hill, 1978), and Constance Backhouse and Leah Cohen, *The Secret Oppression* (Toronto: Macmillan of Canada, 1978).

18. See Richard Sennett and Jonathan Cobb, *The Hidden Injuries of Class* (New York: Random House, 1971), Sar Levitan, *Blue Collar Workers* (New York: McGraw-Hill, 1974), and Patricia Cayo Sexton, *Blue Collars and Hard Hats* (New York: Vintage, 1972).

19. These examples are all true, based on my personal observations.

Chapter Seven

1. Arthur M. Ross and Herbert Hill, *Employment, Race, and Poverty* (New York: Harcourt Brace, 1967), p. 367.

2. Ross and Hill, p. 386. The writer was Will Winn.

3. The unions condemned the Chinese as people "of vice and sexual immorality," the Japanese as having a "leprous mouth."

4. A well-detailed introduction to this history is Judith O'Sullivan and Rosemary Gallick, *Workers and Allies: Female Participation in the American Trade Union Movement, 1824–1976* (Washington, D.C.: U.S. Government, 1976).

5. Eugene V. Schneider, *Industrial Sociology* (New York: McGraw-Hill, 1969).

6. One particularly candid and vivid description of this period is Richard O. Boyer and Herbert M. Morais, *Labor's Untold Story* (New York: United Electrical, Radio, and Machine Workers of America, 1970).

7. Ross and Hill, *Employment*, p. 403.

8. James Kirkpatrick, "Testing and Fair Employment," in Kent Miller and Ralph Mason Dreeger, *Comparative Studies of Blacks and Whites in the U.S.* (New York: Academic Press, 1975).

9. Benjamin Wolkinson, *Black Unions and the EEOC* (Lexington: Lexington Books, 1973).

10. Rosie the Riveter was a rarity even during the war—only about 5 percent of blue collar jobs were held by women during this time.

11. Lucretia M. Dewey, "Women in Labor Unions," *Monthly Labor Review* 94,5 (1971): 2–48. Edna Raphael, "Working Women and Their Membership in Labor Unions," *Monthly Labor Review* 97,5 (1974): 27–33.

12. Barbara Wertheimer and Anne H. Nelson, *Trade Union Women*

(New York: Praeger, 1975). Union leaders blame the women for not being active members rather than examining whether union policies hamper and discourage that participation. Yet more women than men are interested in the unions they belong to, and desire more acceptance and encouragement from leadership. The male leader's attitude is to locate the "right" woman for positions of responsibility, whereas women believe everyone should have more say.

13. Alice H. Cook, "Women and American Trade Unions," *The Annals*, 375 (1968): 124–132. See also Wertheimer and Nelson, *Trade Union Women*. Ninety percent of the skilled workers in the Amalgamated Meat Cutters and Retail Food Employees Union were men. "There is no place for a woman to go after learning to wrap a piece of meat, and there has to be. Life becomes very dull," wrote one. This pattern pervaded the other unions studied.

14. *Working Woman*, March, 1979: 28.

15. U.S. Equal Employment Opportunity Commission, *Minority and Female Membership in Referral Unions*, Research Report No. 55, 1977.

16. Robert W. Hodge, Paul M. Siegel, and Peter H. Rossi, "Occupational Prestige in the United States, 1925–63," *American Journal of Sociology* 70 (1964): 286–302.

17. For further historical detail, see Carol Lopate, *Women in Medicine* (Baltimore: Johns Hopkins University, 1968); James L. Curtis, *Blacks, Medical Schools, and Society* (Ann Arbor: University of Michigan, 1971); Charles E. Odergaard, *Minorities in Medicine* (New York: Josiah Macy, Jr., Foundation, 1977).

18. U.S. Commission on Civil Rights, *Toward Equal Educational Opportunity: Affirmative Action Programs at Law and Medical Schools*, Clearinghouse Publication 55, 1978.

19. These and other recent statistics have been compiled from many sources and published in a resource book on *Professional Women and Minorities*, Scientific Manpower Commission, 1976.

20. These cases are discussed in U.S. Commission on Civil Rights, *Toward Equal Educational Opportunity*, pp. 14–15.

21. This quote is from the transcript of a university committee meeting. Silber later confirmed its accuracy to the *Washington Post*, March 16, 1975.

22. Between 1968 and 1976, white enrollment in medical school increased 49 percent. Black enrollment increased 180 percent, but this figure is deceptive because so few blacks were present to begin with. If you have one black in a school and add another, you have a 100 percent increase. If you have 100 whites and add 49 more, you have 49 percent increase.

23. This hearing is discussed in U.S. Commission on Civil Rights, *Toward Equal Educational Opportunity.*

24. National Research Council, *Science, Engineering, and Humanities Doctorates in the United States, 1977 Profile* (Washington, D.C.: National Academy of Sciences, 1978).

25. Two examples here are Jonathan R. and Stephen Cole, *Social Stratification in Science* (Chicago: University of Chicago Press, 1973) and Jonathan R. Cole, *Fair Science* (New York: Free Press, 1979).

26. Theodore L. Gross, "How to Kill a College," *Saturday Review,* February 4, 1978, pp. 12–20.

Chapter Eight

1. Carl Gersuny, "Devil in Petticoats and Just Cause," *Business History Review* 50 (1976): 131–152; "Work Injuries and Adversary Processes in Two New England Textile Mills," *Business History Review* 51 (1977): 326–340. See also Rebecca Harding Davis, *Life in the Iron Mills* (Old Westbury, Mass.: Feminist Press, 1971).

2. Rosabeth Moss Kanter, *Men and Women of the Corporation* (New York: Basic Books, 1977).

3. The relationship of on-the-job training to human capital is discussed in Robert P. Althauser and Arne L. Kalleberg, "Occupational and Firm Labor Markets," unpublished manuscript, Department of Sociology, Indiana University.

4. Many of these ideas about the relationship of OJT to job ladders were developed by Peter B. Doeringer and Michael Piore, *Internal Labor Markets and Manpower Analysis* (Lexington, Mass.: D. C. Heath, 1971).

5. The "crowding" hypothesis with regard to women was developed by Mary Stevenson, "Relative Wages and Sex Segregation by Occupation," in Cynthia B. Lloyd, *Sex, Discrimination, and the Division of Labor* (New York: Columbia University Press, 1975).

6. The best case study of these differences is Rosabeth Moss Kanter's *Men and Women of the Corporation.*

7. An excellent guide to the "street sense" of playing the promotion game is Betty Lehan Harragan, *Games Your Mother Never Taught You* (New York: Warner, 1977).

8. This section is a brief introduction to "dual labor theory," a recent analysis of the labor market by political economists that has been much ignored within the traditional ranks of the profession. Simultaneously, a few sociologists have challenged traditional social-stratification theory for its failure to recognize that the free labor market is a myth. Among useful sources are Richard Edwards, Michael Reich, and David Gordon, *Labor Market Segmentation* (Lexington, Mass.: Heath, 1974), Sam Rosenberg, "The Marxian Reserve Army of Labor

and the Dual Labor Market," *Politics and Society* 7 (1977): 221–228; Wing-cheung Ng, "The Dual Labor Market Theory: An Evaluation of Its Status in the Field of Ethnic Studies," unpublished paper, Department of Sociology, University of California, Riverside, 1977; Ross M. Stolzenberg, "Occupation Labor Markets and the Process of Wage Attainment," *American Sociological Review* 40 (1975): 645–665; Linda S. Gottfredson, "A Multiple-Labor Market of Occupational Achievement," Report No. 224, and "Occupational Differentiation in the First Decade After High School," Report No. 259, Center for Social Organization of Schools, Johns Hopkins University.

9. Henry Ford, *My Life and Work* (New York: Doubleday, Page, 1922); Anne Jardim, *The First Henry Ford* (Cambridge, Mass.: MIT Press, 1970); Allan Nevins, *Ford* (New York: Scribner, 1954).

10. The movie *With Babies and Banners*, with its superb selection of historic footage from the 1938 strike against General Motors, poignantly documents these events.

11. E. M. Beck, Patrick H. Horan, and Charles M. Tolbert, II, "Stratification in a Dual Economy," *American Sociological Review* 43 (1978): 704–720.

12. For a review of the poor quality of work life, see Special Task Force to the Secretary of Health, Education, and Welfare, *Work in America* (Cambridge, Mass.: MIT Press, 1973).

Chapter Nine

1. Though this chapter focuses on federal patterns, the patterns for state government are similar. See Leo Sigelman, "The Curious Case of Women in State and Local Government," *Social Science Quarterly* 56 (1975): 591–604.

2. James F. Long, "Employment Discrimination in the Federal Sector," *Journal of Human Resources* 11 (1976): 86–97.

3. *U.S. News and World Report*, "Washington Problem: Bias in Own Ranks," May 14, 1979: 74–75.

4. Judy Chase, "Inside HEW: Women Protest Sex Discrimination," *Science* 174 (October 15, 1971): 270–274.

5. R. Lynn Rittenoure, "Measuring Fair Employment Practices," *American Journal of Economics and Sociology* 37 (1978): 113–128.

6. *U.S. News*, "Washington Problem."

7. A thoughtful history of this legislation is Donald Allen Robinson, "Two Movements in Pursuit of Equal Employment Opportunity," *Signs* (1979): 411–433. Representative Martha Griffiths, a shrewd feminist legislator, collaborated with Smith in placing "sex" in Title VII.

8. A useful compendium of federal antidiscrimination regulations is U.S. Commission on Civil Rights, *A Guide to Federal Laws and Regulations Prohibiting Sex Discrimination,* 1976.

9. *U.S. News and World Report,* "Washington Problem."

10. Arthur Fletcher, *The Silent Sell-Off* (New York: Third World Press, 1973).

11. Personal communication from Weldon J. Rougeau, Director, Office of Federal Contract Compliance Programs.

12. United States Department of Labor, Sixty-Sixth Annual Report, Fiscal Year 1978.

13. All banking material in this discussion comes from Rodney Alexander and Elizabeth Supery, *The Shortchanged: Women and Minorities in Banking* (New York: Dunellen, 1973).

14. James J. Heckman and Kenneth I. Wolpin, "Does the Contract Compliance Program Work?" *Industrial and Labor Relations Review* 29 (1976): 544–564.

15. Morris Goldstein and Robert S. Smith, "The Estimated Impact of the Antidiscrimination Program aimed at Federal Contractors," *Industrial and Labor Relations Review* 29 (1976): 523–543. For similar research on the EEOC see Orley Ashenfelter and James Blue, *Evaluating the Labor-Market Effect of Social Programs* (Princeton: Industrial Relations Section, Princeton University, 1976).

16. Robert Flanagan, "Actual Versus Potential Impact of Government Antidiscrimination Programs," *Industrial and Labor Relations Review* 29 (1976): 486–587.

17. Margaret Oppenheimer and Helen La Van, "Comparing Arbitration and Litigation in Employment Discrimination Cases," *Monthly Labor Review* 102 (May 1979): 35–36.

18. Norma B. Chaty, "The Question of Job Bias," *California Living,* November 18, 1979 (Part I) and November 25, 1979 (Part II).

Chapter Ten

1. Lester Thurow, "Inequality, Inflation, and Growth in the American Economy," *The Economist* (December 24, 1977): 31–35.

2. A useful guide here is Betty R. Aderson and Martha P. Rogers, *Personnel Testing and Equal Employment Opportunity,* Equal Employment Opportunity Commission, 1970.

Chapter Eleven

1. U.S. Equal Employment Opportunity Commission, *Promise Versus Performance* (June, 1972). The statements by executives in this report document a gamut of denial, obfuscation, and refusal to take respon-

sibility. If they speak so foolishly in public, one wonders about their private machinations.

2. Lester Thurow, *Investment in Human Capital* (Belmont, Calif.: Wadsworth, 1970).

3. Herbert E. Meyer, "Remodelling the Executive for the Corporate Climb," *Fortune*, July 16, 1979.

4. The restrictiveness of the male sex role is well documented in Jack Nichols, *Men's Liberation* (New York: Penguin, 1975), and Joseph Pleck and Jack Sawyer, Editors, *Men and Masculinity* (Englewood Cliffs, N.J.: Prentice-Hall, 1974).

5. Personal communication, James Wood, Department of Sociology, San Diego State University.

6. For more on this by an experienced personnel expert, see Dean B. Peskin, *The Building Blocks of EEO* (New York: World, 1971).

7. A thoughtful review of this material is Linda Putnam and J. Stephen Heinen, "Women in Management: The Fallacy of the Trait Approach," *MSU Business Topics* (Summer, 1976): 47–53.

8. This reproduction is actually increasing, not decreasing. See Frederick D. Sturdivant and Roy D. Adler, "Executive Origins: Still a Gray Flannel World," *Harvard Business Review* (November-December, 1976): 125–132.

9. Among the various EEOC documents, the most straightforward and revealing is Jerolyn R. Lyle, *Affirmative Action Programs for Women: A Survey of Innovative Programs* (n.d.).

10. Douglas W. Bray, "Identifying Managerial Talent in Women," *Atlanta Economic Review* (March-April, 1976): 38–43.

11. The framework for this outline was inspired by Constance Backhouse and Leah Cohen, *The Secret Oppression: Sexual Harassment of Working Women* (Toronto: Macmillan, 1978), pp. 185–189.

12. One model for such planning is Neil C. Churchill and John K. Shank, "Affirmative Action and Guilt-Edged Goals," *Harvard Business Review* (March-April 1976): 111–116. The writers overlook the possibility of increasing minority and women job candidates by revising job qualifications to accommodate their different work histories. Their proposal would produce faster change were this also implemented.

13. Firms tend to put all their resources into support for the disadvantaged worker, and neglect that established males need guidance and techniques for change.

14. Gloria Steinem, "If Men Could Menstruate," *Ms.*, October, 1978, p. 110.

15. The material following is based upon information provided by Helen Remick, Director of Affirmative Action for Women, University

of Washington. See her unpublished papers, "Strategies for Creating Sound, Bias-Free Job Evaluation Plans," and "Beyond Equal Pay for Equal Work: Comparable Worth in the State of Washington."
16. The consultants were Norman D. Willis & Associates. Their reports are "State of Washington: Comparable Worth Study," (September 1974), and "State of Washington: Comparable Worth Study, Phase II," (December 1976)."

Chapter Twelve

1. Norman B. Chaty, "The Question of Job Bias," *California Living*, November 25, 1979.
2. Christopher Lasch, *The Culture of Narcissism* (New York: Norton, 1979).
3. U.S. Department of Commerce, *Social Indicators: 1976*.
4. Report of a Special Task Force to the Secretary of Health, Education, and Welfare, *Work in America* (Cambridge, Mass.: MIT Press, 1973).

Index

DATE DUE